1000 Civil Aircraft in Colour

Gerry Manning

MIDLAND
An imprint of
Ian Allan Publishing

1000 Civil Aircraft in Colour
© 2005 Gerry Manning

ISBN 1 85780 208 X

Published by Midland Publishing
4 Watling Drive, Hinckley, LE10 3EY, England
Tel: 01455 254 490   Fax: 01455 254 495
E-mail: midlandbooks@compuserve.com

Midland Publishing is an imprint of
Ian Allan Publishing Ltd

Worldwide distribution (except North America):
Midland Counties Publications
4 Watling Drive, Hinckley, LE10 3EY, England
Telephone: 01455 254 450   Fax: 01455 233 737
E-mail: midlandbooks@compuserve.com
www.midlandcountiessuperstore.com

North American trade distribution:
Specialty Press Publishers & Wholesalers Inc.
39966 Grand Avenue, North Branch, MN 55056
Tel: 651 277 1400   Fax: 651 277 1203
Toll free telephone: 800 895 4585
www.specialtypress.com

Design and concept
© 2005 Midland Publishing
Layout by Sue Bushell

Printed in England
by Ian Allan Printing Ltd
Riverdene Business Park, Molesey Road,
Hersham, Surrey, KT12 4RG

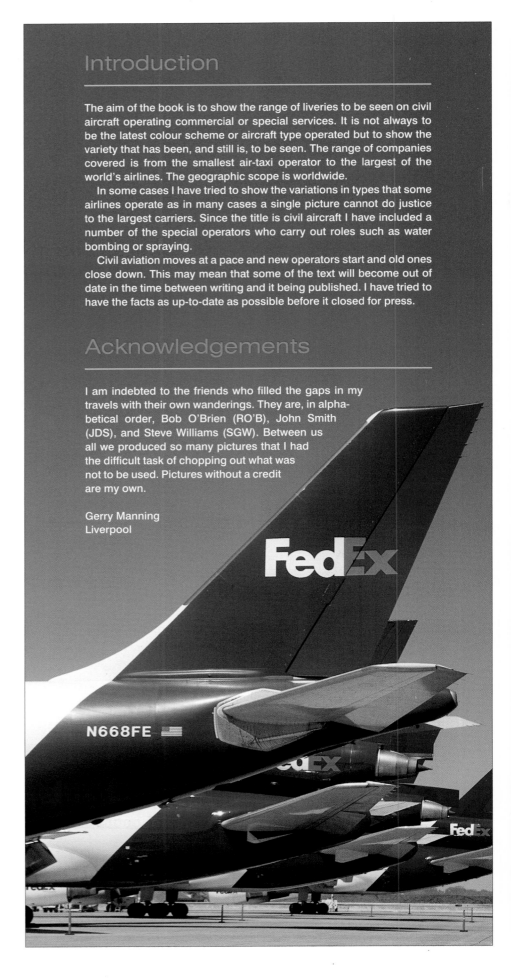

Introduction

The aim of the book is to show the range of liveries to be seen on civil aircraft operating commercial or special services. It is not always to be the latest colour scheme or aircraft type operated but to show the variety that has been, and still is, to be seen. The range of companies covered is from the smallest air-taxi operator to the largest of the world's airlines. The geographic scope is worldwide.

In some cases I have tried to show the variations in types that some airlines operate as in many cases a single picture cannot do justice to the largest carriers. Since the title is civil aircraft I have included a number of the special operators who carry out roles such as water bombing or spraying.

Civil aviation moves at a pace and new operators start and old ones close down. This may mean that some of the text will become out of date in the time between writing and it being published. I have tried to have the facts as up-to-date as possible before it closed for press.

Acknowledgements

I am indebted to the friends who filled the gaps in my travels with their own wanderings. They are, in alphabetical order, Bob O'Brien (RO'B), John Smith (JDS), and Steve Williams (SGW). Between us all we produced so many pictures that I had the difficult task of chopping out what was not to be used. Pictures without a credit are my own.

Gerry Manning
Liverpool

Right: Air Alfa of Istanbul, Turkey, operated a small fleet of Airbus designs. Boeing 727-230 TC-ALM (c/n 20431) was the one exception to this. It is pictured at East Midlands Airport in July 1997. The carrier has been renamed Alfa Airlines.

Below left: The small island state of Aruba hosted Air Aruba. Seen landing at Miami in October 1998, is McDonnell Douglas MD-88 N12FQ (c/n 49766). This leased aircraft was one of two in the fleet of six not to carry the 'P4' registration letter of the nation. On orders from the national government the carrier ceased all operations in October 2000 due to a deteriorating financial situation.

Above right: Seen landing at London-Heathrow in July 1997, is Airbus A310-203 7T-VJD (c/n 293) of Air Algerie. This carrier is the flag carrier for Algeria and has a mixed fleet, ranging from agricultural aircraft to Boeing 767s.

Left: Air Algerie's cargo operations are handled by a pair of Lockheed 382G Hercules transports. 7T-VHG (c/n 51c-4880) is pictured landing at Frankfurt in June 1999.

Below left: Australian Airlines is a subsidiary of Qantas and based in the northern part of Queensland at Cairns. It operates long-haul low-cost international services around Asia. Boeing 767-338(ER) VH-OGI (c/n 25246) is seen at base in February 2003.

Above right: Air Botnia is a Finnish passenger carrier flying mainly domestic routes but with some international operations. BAe 3201 Jetstream 32 OH-JAB (c/n 835) is seen at Kuopto in June 1998 with its TPE331 turbo props running before departing on a local flight to the capital Helsinki. The airline is now known as Blue 1.

Left: With a most distinctive colour scheme, Portuguese charter operator Air Columbus flew holidaymakers from and to its Madeira base until operations were suspended at the end of 1994. Boeing 737-33A CS-TKD (c/n 23830) is pictured landing at Manchester in May 1992.

Based in the capital Brussels, **Air Belgium** was owned by UK holiday company Airtours. Boeing 737-46B OO-ILJ (c/n 25262) is seen at Manchester in April 1998. All operations ceased in October 2000.

Air Bosna is from Bosnia-Herzegovina, once part of Yugoslavia. International operations to western Europe originate from the capital Sarajevo. Yakovlev Yak-42 T9-ABC (c/n 11151004) is seen at Düsseldorf in September 1998.

Above: With a fleet of 100-plus freighters **Airborne Express** of Wilmington, Ohio is one of the bigger US parcel cargo airlines. Douglas DC-8-63 N820AX (c/n 46155) is seen on the move at Phoenix, Arizona in October 1998.

Below: Latvian operator **Air Baltic** flies Western designs for their services. Avro RJ70 YL-BAK (c/n E1223) is seen at Frankfurt in June 1997.

Above: Canadian commuter carrier **Air BC** was a subsidiary of Air Canada and flew services from its base at Vancouver. BAe 146-200A C-FBAO (c/n E2111) is seen arriving at Edmonton, Alberta in May 2000.

Air Europa is a Spanish scheduled and charter operator with a fleet of nearly forty Boeing 737 and 767 aircraft. Boeing 737-81Q EC-ICD (c/n 30785) is pictured landing at Madrid in September 2002. It is one of the fleet that has been fitted with winglets.

Air Europa Express is a sister company of Air Europa and flies scheduled services with a fleet of BAe ATPs around Spain. EC-GSF (c/n 2039) is seen retracting its wheels after take-off from Palma, Majorca in September 2000.

Dutch charter carrier **Air Holland** operated an all-Boeing fleet before it went into receivership in November 1999. Boeing 757-27B PH-AHI (c/n 24137) is seen at the then company base of Amsterdam-Schiphol in August 1997.

An all-freight operator, **Air Colombia** is based at Villavicencio with just two aircraft. Douglas DC-6A HK-4046X (c/n 43708) is seen at base in September 1997.

Swiss tour operator Prishtina Reisen operates Airbus A320-211 HB-IJZ (c/n 211) with the titles **Air Prishtina**. It is pictured just a week after the start of operations in September 2004 at Zürich.

Above: Aerovip is an Argentine commuter operator with a fleet of seven 19-seat Jetstreams. Seen at its base, Buenos Aires – Aeroparque J Newbery, in October 2003, is BAe 3201 Jetstream 32EP LV-ZRL (c/n 928).

Below: Air Berlin is a growing German passenger carrier based at that city's Tegel Airport. The majority of the fleet comprises over forty Boeing 737s. Photographed is one of three Fokker 100s operated. D-AGPE (c/n 11300) is seen at base in May 2004.

Above: N54514 Curtiss C-46D Commando (c/n 33285) is operated by Fairbanks, Alaska-based **Air Cargo Express**. It has nose art and the name 'Maid in Japan', a reference to the airframe's former history in the Japanese military. It was photographed, at base, in May 2000.

Right: With a history dating back to 1933, **Air France** can claim to be amongst the world's oldest airlines. Pictured at Beijing in October 1999, is Boeing 777-228 F-GSPF (c/n 29007).

Following the first fatal crash of the type in July 2000, **Air France** withdrew their Concorde fleet from service. Pictured at Zürich in August 1998, on a flight to celebrate 50 years of the airport is BAe/Aérospatiale Concorde 101 F-BVFB (c/n 207).

Air Canada uses over seventy Airbus A319 and A320 aircraft for services around North America. A320-211 C-FKCK (c/n 265) is seen at Edmonton, Alberta in May 2000.

With a fifty-seat capacity the Canadair Regional Jet is popular with **Air Canada** for many routes. RJ100ER C-FWJF (c/n 7095) is seen operating an international service to Minneapolis-St Paul in May 2000.

Following the takeover of Canadian, **Air Canada** has become the main carrier for that nation. Seen landing at Zürich in August 1998, is Airbus A340-313 C-GBQM (c/n 216). This type is used for long-haul international services.

Air China operates both Boeing and Airbus designs. Airbus A340-313 B-2387 (c/n 201) is pictured about to touch down on Runway 28 at Zürich in August 1998.

The largest of China's many airlines is **Air China**. With new western equipment and excellent cabin service it flies both international and domestic routes. Boeing 777-2J6 B-2063 (c/n 29156) is pictured at its Beijing base in October 1999.

The BAe 146-100 is used by **Air China** in 82-seat configuration. B-2710 (c/n E1085) awaits its next passenger load at Guangzhou in October 1999.

Air China Cargo operates five dedicated 747 freighters for cargo services. Boeing 747-2J6F B-2462 (c/n 24960) is seen arriving at Frankfurt in June 1999.

Russian carrier Aeroflot, following the break up of the Soviet Union, is now a dedicated international carrier. It used to cover every single civil aircraft in that vast country. Largest of the Russian-built passenger airliners is the Ilyushin IL-96-300; note the winglets. RA-96011 (c/n 74393201008) is seen on the move at Bangkok in February 2001.

The thought of an Aeroflot Boeing would have been unthinkable only a few years ago. Boeing 777-2Q8 VP-BAS (c/n 27607) is seen at Beijing in October 1999, in the colour scheme of Aeroflot's leased western aircraft.

In the traditional Aeroflot livery is Antonov An-124-100 RA-82070 at Sharjah, UAE, in March 1997. This freighter is the world's largest production aircraft with a weight of over 400 tons.

Above: Airbus provided the first western aircraft to Aeroflot. Airbus A310-308 F-OGQT (c/n 622) is seen at London-Heathrow in July 1993, in a new, but short-lived, scheme.

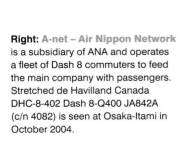

Right: A-net – Air Nippon Network is a subsidiary of ANA and operates a fleet of Dash 8 commuters to feed the main company with passengers. Stretched de Havilland Canada DHC-8-402 Dash 8-Q400 JA842A (c/n 4082) is seen at Osaka-Itami in October 2004.

The perfect name for a Chinese airline has to be **Air Great Wall**. With a fleet of three 737s it flies internal services from the company base at Ningbo. Boeing 737-2T4 B-2507 (c/n 23273) is seen arriving at Beijing in October 1999. The carrier was merged into China Eastern Airlines in 2002.

Formed in 1999, **Air Gulf Falcon** is based at Sharjah, UAE. It flies cargo 707s and passenger 747s. The aircraft are registered in either Equatorial Guinea (3C) or Swaziland (3D). Boeing 707-307C 3D-SGF (c/n 19999) is seen at base in March 2000. Operations were transferred to Sky Aviation in 2001.

Aeromas is a small mixed passenger and freight carrier based in the capital of Uruguay, Montevideo. EMB-110P1 Bandeirante CX-MAS (c/n 11033) is the largest in the fleet. It is pictured at base in October 2003.

Flying holiday charters from Manchester and London-Gatwick is British carrier **Astraeus** with a fleet of seven 148-seat Boeings. Pictured at Manchester in June 2002 is Boeing 737-3S3 G-STRA (c/n 24059) departing from Runway 24L.

Left: Air Georgia became one of the airlines founded in the new republic of that name following the collapse of the Soviet Union. Tupolev Tu-154B-2 4L-AAH (c/n 558) is pictured at Frankfurt in June 1999. At the start of 2000 the carrier merged into Air Zena/Georgian Airlines based in the capital Tbilisi.

Below: Spanish commuter carrier **Air Nostrum** flies as Iberia Regional and in a variant of the flag carrier's livery. Fokker 50 EC-GKX (c/n 20275) departs into the blue sky of Palma, Majorca in September 2000.

An all-freight carrier, **Air Hong Kong** has been operating since 1986. Boeing 707-336C VR-HKK (c/n 20517) is seen on a regular scheduled service to Manchester in July 1990.

India's international flag carrier is **Air India**. Founded in 1948 it flies worldwide passenger services. Airbus A310-304 VT-EQS (c/n 538) arrives at Manchester in April 1998.

Lisbon-based **Air Luxor** operates both long- and short-haul passenger charter flights. Airbus A320-211 CS-TQH (c/n 023) is seen at Rome in September 2004.

Albarka Air is a Nigerian passenger carrier based in the federal capital, Abuja. BAC One-Eleven 520FN 5N-BBQ (c/n 230) is pictured in store at Luqa, Malta in September 2004. It carries extra titles proclaiming it to be the official carrier for the Miss World contest, held in Nigeria in 2001.

Above: Air Inter was a French scheduled passenger carrier. Airbus A320-211 F-GHQK (c/n 236) is pictured landing at London-Heathrow in June 1996. In September the following year the airline, owned by Air France, was merged into the parent company.

Below: In a livery that reflects its exotic base, **Air Jamaica** operates three twin-aisle Airbus aircraft. A340-312 6Y-JMC (c/n 048) is seen at London-Heathrow in July 1999.

Above: Air Atlanta Icelandic has a large fleet of Boeing 747, 757 and 767 aircraft that it operates either for itself or on short-term ACMI (Aircraft, Crew, Maintenance, Insurance) contracts for other carriers. Boeing 747-267B TF-ATC (c/n 22149) is seen at Manchester in August 2003. It carries 'Air Atlanta Europe' titles.

Left: Air Koryo is the sole airline in the Democratic People's Republic of Korea (North Korea). Only limited international services are operated. Ilyushin IL-62M P-881 (c/n 3647853) is seen arriving at Bangkok in November 1999.

Flag carrier for Sri Lanka was **Air Lanka**, based in the capital Colombo. Airbus A340-311 4R-ADC (c/n 034) arrives at Frankfurt in June 1999. The carrier was renamed Srilankan Airlines the following month.

Miami-based **Airlift International** was a famous DC-8 cargo carrier, which also operated some services with Friendships. Fairchild FH-227C N374RD (c/n 504) is seen at base in June 1989. The carrier suspended operations in 1992.

French passenger carrier **Air Liberté** Airbus A300-622R F-GHEG (c/n 569) is pictured on approach to Runway 24 at Manchester in June 1996, full of football supporters for the Euro '96 tournament. The following September the airline went into receivership and was sold.

Air Liberté was purchased by British Airways and continued operations from its Paris-Orly base. The new owners had the fleet repainted in the BA World Image livery with different tail marks. McDonnell Douglas MD-83 F-GHHO (c/n 49985) is seen landing in early evening sun at Palma, Majorca in September 2000. This tail design *is l'esprit liberté* and shows text from the declaration of human rights. Under new owners it was renamed Air Lib in September 2001.

Flag carrier for the Republic of Seychelles is **Air Seychelles**. Boeing 767s are used for long-haul operations as well as a number of commuter types for inter-island flights. Britten-Norman BN-2A Trislander S7-AAN (c/n 1026) is seen at the capital Mahé in June 1983. (RO'B)

California commuter operator **Air Pacific** de Havilland Canada DHC-6 Twin Otter 300 N127AP (c/n 289) is pictured at Merced, California in October 1979. Early the following year the carrier merged into Gem State Airlines.

Another **Air Pacific** is a Fiji-based passenger carrier. It operates international services from its Pacific island location. Boeing 737-7X2 DQ-FJF (c/n 28878) is seen on such a flight at Melbourne-Tullamarine, Australia in February 2003.

Canadian commuter carrier **Air Ontario** flew services for Air Canada around the province. De Havilland Canada DHC-8 Dash 8-102 C-FGQI (c/n 185) is ready to roll at base, London Ontario, June 1990.

Above: Rome-based passenger carrier **Air One** operates a fleet of 737s with aircraft registered in several European countries. Boeing 737-230 I-JETC (c/n 23153) is seen on a domestic flight at Naples in September 2004.

Left: National flag carrier **Air Zimbabwe** flies services from the capital Harare. Boeing 767-2N0(ER) Z-WPE (c/n 24713) is seen at Frankfurt in June 1999. Note that the registration has a total of only four letters.

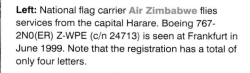

Spanish passenger carrier **Air Plus Comet** has a mixed Boeing/Airbus fleet. Airbus A310-325(ET) EC-HIF (c/n 624) is seen landing at the company base, Madrid, in September 2002.

Above: Aussie Air is a small Australian carrier, based in Adelaide, with a fleet of just two aircraft. Cessna 402B VH-BIZ (c/n 402B-0622) is seen at Avalon in February 2003.

Right: Air Portugal – TAP is the national flag carrier with an all-Airbus fleet. Smallest is the single-aisle A319 with 132 seats. A319-111 CS-TTB (c/n 755) is seen at Frankfurt in June 1999.

Largest aircraft in the **Air Portugal – TAP** fleet is the four-engine, twin-aisle A340. Airbus A340-312 CS-TOB (c/n 044) approaches to land on Runway 09L at London-Heathrow in July 1999.

Based at Kazan in the Russian republic of Tatarstan, **Air Stan** operates an all-cargo airline. Ilyushin IL-76TD RA-76842 (c/n 1033418616) is seen awaiting loading at Stansted in August 1999.

Air Spray of Red Deer, Alberta, is a Canadian company specialising in flying tanker aircraft to combat forest fires. Lockheed L-188A Electra C-FQYB (c/n 1063) is seen at base in May 2000. The company is one of the few operators of the pure Electra tanker. Some US operators fly the converted Orion, which is of course a development of the Electra.

Air Spray also operate eighteen Douglas Invaders, a World War Two light bomber, in tanker roles. A-26C (B-26C) C-FPGP (c/n 29177) is seen at the company base of Red Deer in May 2000 before going to its summer 'air attack' base.

Above left: American commuter operator **Air Sunshine's** largest aircraft is the fifteen-seat Bandeirante. Pictured at the company base of Fort Lauderdale Florida, on an untypical day for the location in October 1998 is Embraer EMB-110P Bandeirante N123HY (c/n 110321).

Above right: Seen in late-evening sunshine at its Bogota base in September 1997, is **Avianca** Boeing 767-259 N985AN (c/n 24618). This Colombian operator flies long-haul international services as well as domestic.

Left: **Avianca** operate a fleet of ten Fokker 50s for internal services. All are leased, hence the Dutch registrations. PH-MXS (c/n 20299) is seen at Bogota in September 1997.

Right: Italian regional operator **Air Dolomiti** is based at Trieste and is a subsidiary of German carrier Lufthansa. ATR 72-500 I-ADLT (c/n 638) is seen at Frankfurt in June 2001.

Below: Based at Denpasar, on the Indonesian holiday island of Bali is **Air Paradise International**. With a fleet of two Airbus widebodies it flies regional international services. Airbus A300-622R PK-KDK (c/n 633) is seen at Australia's Sydney-Kingsford Smith Airport in October 2004. (RO'B)

Above: Manchester-based **Air Scandic** operated two Airbus wide bodies and specialises in sub-leases to holiday charter operators. A300B4-203FF G-SWJW (c/n 302) is seen departing base in June 2002.

Above: Manchester-based **Airtours** is one of the largest European holiday charter operators. Boeing 757-225 G-RJGR (c/n 22197) is seen being pushed back from Manchester's Terminal 1 in parallel with another at the start of a service in May 1998. The company now operate under the name MyTravel.

Below: To handle long-haul holiday charters **Airtours** leased this Air New Zealand 747 during 1998. Note the livery is an amalgam of both carriers. Boeing 747-219B ZK-NZZ (c/n 22791) is pictured at Manchester in May 1998.

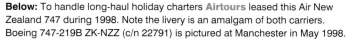

Above: With a fleet of over one hundred small cargo aircraft **Ameriflight** are to be found at many western state cities loading freight. Beech 1900C Airliner N330AF (c/n UB-38) is seen with its freight door open at Oxnard, California in October 2001.

Below: Montreal-based **Air Transat** fly Atlantic charters with both single- and twin-aisle aircraft. Boeing 757-236 C-GTSJ (c/n 24772) is seen at Amsterdam-Schiphol in October 1999.

Left: Largest aircraft in the **Air Transat** fleet is the twin-engined Airbus A330. Seen landing at Manchester in June 2000, is A330-243 C-GGTS (c/n 250).

Below: **Andes Airlines** was an Ecuadorean freight carrier based at Guayaquil. Canadair CL-44-6 HC-AZH (c/n 13) is seen stored at base in September 1997. This airframe is an ex-RCAF CC-106 Yukon and does not have the swing tail. The airline ceased operations the following year.

Above left: **Air Tindi** is based at Yellowknife in Canada's North West Territory. It operates a fleet of assorted types providing an ad-hoc air service to the scattered communities of that vast landmass. De Havilland Canada DHC-3 Turbo Otter C-FXUY (c/n 142) is seen at base in May 2000. The original piston engine has been replaced with a PT6A turboprop.

Left: Pictured at Dublin in June 1994, is Antonov An-124-100 Ruslan UR-82066 (c/n 19530502761) operated by **Antonov Air Cargo Operations**. This company is part of the Antonov Design Bureau.

Below left: The Antonov An-32P is the ultimate development from the An-24. The engine power is twice the original, the powerplants being mounted over the wings. UR-48086 (c/n 2901) is a water-bomber conversion owned by the **Antonov OKB** (Design Bureau). It is pictured at Moscow-Zhukovsky in August 1995.

Above: **AECA** (Aeroservicios Ecuatorianos CA) is an Ecuadorean freight airline based at Guayaquil. Boeing 707-321C HC-BGP (c/n 19273) is seen on the ramp at Manta on the country's Pacific coast in September 1997.

Left: Once known as Flight West Airlines, **Alliance Airlines** took its current name in July 2002. Based in Brisbane, the Australian passenger carrier has a fleet of two Fokker 100s. VH-FWI (c/n 11318) is seen at base in February 2003.

Convair CV-580 YV-969C (c/n 150) is operated by Caracas-based **Air Venezuela**. It is pictured at base, November 1997. Operations were suspended in 2001. (RO'B)

Airworld was a UK charter operator owned by holiday company Thomas Cook. Airbus A320-214 G-BXTA (c/n 764) is seen on approach to London-Gatwick in August 1998. Later that year they merged into Flying Colours.

Air 2000 used to be the operating airline for First Choice Holidays. Boeing 767-38A (ER) G-OOAL (c/n 29617) is seen departing Manchester in August 2003. Early in 2004 they changed their name to First Choice Airways.

Above: British regional airline **Air UK** flew both domestic and international services. Fokker F.27 Friendship 200 G-BHMY (c/n 10196) is seen at London-Heathrow in October 1993. KLM, who had a share in the company, enlarged this until they totally owned the carrier. They then flew as KLM uk.

Left: **Air 2000** Boeing 757-225 G-OOOV (c/n 22211) heads a line of four sister ships at Manchester's Terminal 2 in June 1996. They are in the airline's original scheme.

Below left: **ATA – American Trans Air** has a fleet of over eighty jet airliners of three types. Boeing 727-227 N778AT (c/n 22005) taxies to the gate at Phoenix, Arizona in October 1998 in the carrier's old livery.

Pictured arriving at London-Gatwick in August 1998, is **ATA – American Trans Air** Lockheed TriStar 100 N198AT L-1011 (c/n 1111). This picture shows off the new colours adopted by the Indianapolis-based carrier.

Left: Asiana is one of South Korea's two main passenger airlines. It flies both domestic and international services. Seen on the latter is Airbus A321-231 HL7590 (c/n 1060) as it lands at Guangzhou in southern China in October 1999.

Below: Flying this short-body Boeing 727 in a cargo-only role is Bogota, Colombia-based **Aero Sucre**. Boeing 727-59F HK-727 (c/n 19127) is seen on the ramp at base in September 1997.

Irish Commuter carrier **Aer Arann** operates both ATR 42 and 72 aircraft on domestic and international services. ATR 42-300 EI-CVS (c/n 032) is seen lined up to depart at Manchester in July 2004.

Air Andaman was a regional Thai passenger carrier based in the capital Bangkok. Fokker 50 HS-KLD (c/n 20188) is seen at base in October 2003. The carrier ceased operations in February of the following year with the intention of restarting operations. (RO'B)

Above: Seen being loaded with cargo at Miami in October 1998, is **American International Airways** Douglas DC-8F-55 N6161M (c/n 45762). It is in the carrier's full livery. In March the following year the company was renamed Kitty Hawk International.

Right: Spanish holiday charter carrier **Aviaco** was owned by Iberia. Douglas DC-8-52 EC-ATP (c/n 45658) is at Palma, Majorca in November 1974. The airline was merged into the parent company in September 1999.

Allegheny Commuter Shorts 360 N360SA (c/n SH3601) is seen on the move at Washington National (DC) in May 1989. The carrier flew services for US Air and most aircraft were repainted with US Air Express titles.

Russian carrier Avia Energo flies a mix of passenger and cargo types. Like so many airlines in that country they have wonderful liveries. Tupolev Tu-154M RA-85798 (c/n 982) is seen on the ramp at Moscow-Vnukovo in August 1995.

Above left: Based at Moscow-Myachkovo Atran-Aviatrans is an all-cargo airline. Antonov An-32 RA-48109 (c/n 1708) is seen at base in August 1995.

Above right: Pictured landing at Zürich, August 1998, is Boeing 737-53C F-GINL (c/n 24827) of French passenger carrier AOM (Air Outre Mer). The airline was a holiday charter company. It was merged into Air Lib in September 2001.

Right: AMSA (Aerolineas Mundo SA) was a cargo line in the Dominican Republic. Curtiss C-46A Commando HI-495CT (c/n 261) is seen on the ramp at the company base, Santo Domingo, in November 1992. The airline suspended services in 1997.

ACES (Aerolineas Centrales de Colombia) flies both international and domestic services from its Medellin base. ATR 42-320 HK-3684X (c/n 284) is on the ramp at base in November 1992. Note the policeman with sniffer dog by the nose of the aircraft. They are looking for one of the best-known exports from the town.

Seen arriving at Miami in October 1998, in the carrier's new livery is ACES Airbus A320-233 VP-BVA (c/n 739). Like many leased aircraft it has not taken up a Colombian registration.

Aero Union of Chico, California is one of the companies in the forefront of water-bombing operations. This is both as an operator of a fleet of air tankers and as a manufacturer of tanks and converting the aircraft equipped with them. Lockheed P-3A Orion N927AU (c/n 185-5082) is seen at base in October 2001.

This Boeing 377-MG Mini Guppy N422AU (c/n 15937) was used by Aero Union for bulk freight work. The Guppy is a conversion of the Boeing Stratocruiser as an outsize cargo aircraft first used in the early days of the US space program. It is seen at its Chico base in September 1988.

Above: Fast-growing US domestic passenger carrier America West is based at Phoenix, Arizona. Boeing 737-3Q8 N327AW (c/n 23507) is pictured at base in October 1998.

Below: America West's commuter services operate under the name America West Express. The aircraft are owned and operated by Mesa Airlines and fly in America West Express colours. Canadair Regional Jet RJ200LR N7264V (c/n 7264) is seen at Phoenix in October 1998.

Based at Buenos Aires-Aeroparque J Newbery, scheduled passenger carrier Austral is now owned by Aerolineas Argentinas. BAC One-Eleven 521FH LV-JNT (c/n 196) is seen at base when still operated as an independent in June 1994. (RO'B)

Above: Air Nauru is the sole airline in the Pacific republic of the same name. Boeing 727-77C C2-RN4 (c/n 20370) is seen at Melbourne in February 1981, at the end of an international flight to Australia. (RO'B)

Left: AIRES (Aerovias de Integracion Regional SA) is a Colombian commuter operator. De Havilland Canada DHC-8 Dash 8-301 HK-3951X (c/n 184) is seen at its Bogota base in September 1997.

British carrier **AB Airlines** evolved from Air Bristol. Boeing 737-33A G-OABA (c/n 24097) is seen landing at London-Gatwick in August 1998. The airline ceased operations in September of the following year.

Above: Air Florida was based at Miami. It flew both domestic and international passenger services. Boeing 737-222 N63AF (c/n 19553) is seen at Tampa, Florida in October 1981. The carrier later merged with Midway.

Left: Turkish carrier **Akdeniz Airlines** was founded in 1995 and ceased services later the same year. Airbus A300B4-103 N16982 (c/n 091) is seen in store at Tucson, Arizona in October 1998.

Below: Egyptian passenger carrier **AMC** (Air Maintenance Company) is based at Cairo. McDonnell Douglas MD-90-30 SU-BMQ (c/n 53576) is seen at Frankfurt in June 1999.

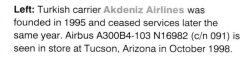

Above: Aviateca Guatemala is the national flag carrier for the Central American country. Douglas DC-8-61 N30UA (c/n 45888) is seen at Miami in June 1989, on lease to the airline.

Right: Operating a fleet of three Caribou freighters from Madrid-Cuatro Vientos was **Avinsa Lineas Aereas**. Photographed at base, in September 2002, is DHC-4A Caribou EC-GQL (c/n 258). Operations were suspended the following year.

Above: Austrian flag carrier **Austrian Airlines** operates Airbus designs ranging from A319 to A340. Seen on a local flight to Zürich in August 1998, is A310-324 OE-LAA (c/n 489).

Turkish carrier **Anatolia** previously operated under the name GTI Airlines. Seen at Zürich in August 1998, is Airbus A300B4-2C TC-ONV (c/n 057).

Below: Seen at one of the furthest reaches of their route network is **Austrian Airlines** A330-223 OE-LAM (c/n 223). It is pictured at Beijing in October 1999.

Colombian operator **Ades – Aerolineas del Este** has as its largest aircraft the Douglas DC-3, the rest of the fleet are single-engined Cessna types. HK-1149 (c/n 26593) is pictured at the company base, Villavicencio in September 1997.

Largest aircraft in the fleet of Peruvian carrier **Aero Transporte SA** is Antonov An-26B-100 OB-1778P (c/n 14205). This aircraft is used for both passenger and freight in a combi role. It is pictured at its Lima base in October 2003.

Above: Arrow Air was a Miami-based all-freight carrier. They had a fleet of DC-8 and L-1011 aircraft. Lockheed L-1011 TriStar 200F N307GB (c/n 1131) is seen on approach to base in October 1998. The company was merged into Fine Air in January 2001.

Left: The Republic of Macedonia is one of the 'new' countries formed following the break-up of Yugoslavia. Based in the capital, Skopje, is **Avioimpex** with a mixed western and ex-Soviet fleet. Yakovlev Yak-42D RA-42389 (c/n 4520424016542) is seen at Zürich in June 1997. This leased aircraft has not been reregistered with the 'Z3' prefix of the country. (JDS)

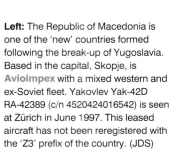

Based at Bogota, Colombian freight airline **ATC** (Aero Transcolombiana de Carga SA) had a fleet of three DC-8s. Douglas DC-8-51F N507DC (c/n 45855) is seen at base in September 1997. Operations were suspended in 2002.

Above: **Alliance Air** was a joint venture between South African Airlines and the governments of Tanzania and Uganda. It was based in the capital of the latter, Entebbe. Boeing 747SP-44 ZS-SPA (c/n 21132) is seen at London-Heathrow in June 1998. Operations ceased in October 2000.

Left: AVENSA (Aerovias Venezolanas SA) has a long history dating back to 1943. Boeing 727-281 YV-95C (c/n 20878) is seen at the airline's Caracas, Venezuela base in November 1992.

Below: Austro Aereo SA is an Ecuadorean passenger carrier based at Cuenca. Fairchild FH-227B HC-BXC (c/n 533) is seen at Quito in September 1997.

With a fleet of just a single DC-3 **Alcom** (Aerolineas Comerciales del Meta) is one of many Colombian carriers based at Villavicencio. Douglas DC-3 HK-4045 (c/n 25808) is seen at base, September 1997.

Air New Zealand is the national flag carrier. They fly both long- and short-haul domestic and international services. Boeing 747-419 ZK-NBU (c/n 25605) is seen at Frankfurt in June 1999.

Smallest aircraft in the fleet of **Air New Zealand** is the 737. Seen following a flight across the Tasman Sea to Melbourne, Australia in February 2003 is Boeing 737-36Q ZK-NGB (c/n 29140)

Above: The second airline of Israel is **Arkia**. It flies both schedule and charter operations. Seen at Frankfurt, in June 1999, is Boeing 757-236 4X-BAZ (c/n 24121).

Based in Swaziland, **African International Airways** operates four cargo aircraft. Douglas DC-8-54F 3D-AFR (c/n 45802) is seen landing at Stansted in August 1999.

Below: With a fleet of 737 and A320 aircraft **Air Malta** serves Europe and the Middle East. Boeing 737-3H9 YU-ANI (c/n 23416) is seen at Frankfurt in June 1997, on a lease from JAT.

Above: Canadian operator **Air North** is based at Whitehorse, Yukon Territory, flying mainly domestic services. Pictured at Fairbanks Alaska, in May 2000 is Hawker Siddeley (Avro) 748-276 Srs.2A C-FAGI (c/n 1699) operating an international scheduled flight.

Left: Seen landing in late evening sun at Anchorage in May 2000, is **Alaska Airlines** Boeing 737-290C N730AS (c/n 22577). The base for this scheduled passenger carrier is in Seattle, Washington, rather than in the state of its name.

Japanese carrier **Air Do – Hokkaido International Airlines** is based in the northern city of Sapporo. It flies a fleet of three 767s in an all-economy seating configuration. Boeing 767-33A(ER) JA98AD (c/n 27476) is seen at Tokyo-Haneda in October 2004.

Showing off its very smart livery at its Bogota base in September 1997, is Colombian passenger carrier **Aero Republica**. Pictured is Douglas DC-9-31 HK-3905X (c/n 47399).

Former Soviet state Azerbaijan now has its own carrier, Azerbaijan Airlines. The majority of the fleet are Russian-built aircraft. Tupolev Tu-154M 4K-AZ10 (c/n 1013) is a VIP aircraft and is seen at London-Heathrow in February 2000.

Above: The growing trend of the low-cost carrier has arrived in Asia. One of the first was Kuala Lumpur, Malaysia-based Air Asia. Boeing 737-301 9M-AAJ (c/n 23511) is seen at Singapore-Changi in September 2004. (RO'B)

Left: German commuter operator Augsburg Airways has some of its fleet of Dash 8s in Team Lufthansa marks. In Augsburg's own livery is de Havilland Canada DHC-8 Dash 8-103 D-BIRT (c/n 260); it is seen at Frankfurt in June 1999.

Right: ASA – African Safari Airways operates a single aircraft on holiday charters. McDonnell Douglas DC-10-30 5Y-MBA (c/n 46952) is seen arriving at Frankfurt in June 1999.

Below: Formed in 1998 Bangkok-based Angel Air operated until their demise in 2003. They first operated leased Malaysian-registered aircraft and later Chinese. Airbus A300-622R B-2323 (c/n 739) is seen at base in February 2001.

Dublin-based Aer Turas has been flying charters since 1962. Cargo-configured Douglas DC-8-63F EI-CGO (c/n 45924) is seen at base in June 1994. The company suspended operations in 2003.

Italian flag carrier **Alitalia** flies worldwide services from Rome. Boeing 767-33A I-DEIL (c/n 28147) is seen at Beijing in October 1999.

Above: Agro Air was an American/Dominican Republic cargo carrier. Douglas DC-8-55F N225VV (c/n 45765) is pictured at the airline's Miami base in June 1989. The company was associated with Fine Air and now flies under that name.

Left: Milan, Italy-based **Azzurra Air** flies regional services for Alitalia with many aircraft in the livery of the flag carrier. Showing its own marks is leased Avro RJ85 EI-CNI (c/n E2299) at Zürich in June 1997. (JDS)

Above: Japanese domestic passenger carrier **Air Nippon** is an associate company with ANA. Seen at Fukuoka in May 1992, is locally-built NAMC YS-11-102 JA8650 (c/n 2013). Two Rolls-Royce Dart turboprops power this airliner. (RO'B)

The ex-Soviet Republic of Moldova now boasts a number of air transport operators. **Air Moldova International** Yakovlev Yak-42D ER-42409 (c/n 4520421216709) is seen at Frankfurt in June 1999.

Below: Tokyo-based **All Nippon Airways** flies both domestic and international services. Boeing 777-281 JA705A (c/n 29029) is seen at Beijing in October 1999.

Air Moldova is associated with Air Moldova International but has a totally different livery. Tupolev Tu-134A-3 ER-65791 (c/n 63110) is pictured at Frankfurt in June 1999.

Adria Airways is based in Ljubljana, Slovenia, formerly part of Yugoslavia. Canadair Regional Jet RJ200LR S5-AAD (c/n 7166) is pictured landing at Zürich in August 1998.

Above: Airbus Transport International is owned by the airliner manufacturer Airbus to move large components between factories. A300-608ST Beluga F-GSTC (c/n 765/3) is pictured at Avalon, Australia, whilst on charter to Eurocopter in February 2003.

Below: Air Niugini is the main flag carrier for the state of Papua New Guinea. The majority of the services are domestic with some regional international ones. Fokker F.28-4000 Fellowship P2-AND (c/n 11118) is pictured at Cairns, Australia in February 2003.

Above: Based in the Channel Island of Guernsey, **Aurigny Air Services** provide an inter-island service as well as flights to the UK mainland. SAAB SF340A G-RUNG (c/n 340A-086) is seen at Manchester in April 2004.

Right: Avesca Colombia (Aerovias Especiales de Carga) flew this smart short-body 727 from Bogota. Boeing 727-11 HK-3770X (c/n 19242) climbs out of base in November 1992. The carrier was renamed Aerocar in June 1994.

Below: Aerotaca of Colombia is a commuter passenger carrier. De Havilland Canada DHC-6 Twin Otter 300 HK-3523 (c/n 608) is seen at the company base of Bogota in September 1997.

One of the nation's two major carriers, **Aeromexico** flies domestic and international services from their base at Mexico City. Douglas DC-9-32 XA-DEM (c/n 47609) is seen at Phoenix, Arizona in October 1998.

Based at Frankfurt, Aero Lloyd was a German regional passenger carrier. Airbus A321-231 D-ALAN (c/n 1218) is seen departing Palma, Majorca in September 2000. In October 2003 they ceased operations and have since restarted under the name Aero Flight.

Above: Atlas Air is an Iranian all-freight company based at the capital Tehran, with a fleet of four IL-76s. Pictured on the ramp at Sharjah, UAE in March 2000, is Ilyushin IL-76TD EP-ALE (c/n 0043453575).

Below: Pictured on the move at its Villavicencio base in September 1997, is Colombian Douglas DC-3 HK-1503 (c/n 34331). It is operated by Aerovanguardia, a local service operator with a fleet of three aircraft.

Alfa Helicopteros is a small Chilean operator with a fleet of four. Sud SA316B Alouette III CC-CRO (c/n 2239) is pictured about to lift off at the company base of Santiago-Tobalaba in October 2003.

Left: Caracas-based Aereotuy is a regional commuter line. De Havilland Canada DHC-6 Twin Otter 300 YV-531C (c/n 528) is seen at base in November 1992. The company now operate under the name LTA – Linea Turistica Aereotuy.

Below left: Aerovilla of Villavicencio, Colombia has a fleet of just one aircraft. Douglas DC-3 HK-3292 (c/n 19661) is pictured receiving maintenance at base in September 1997.

Below right: Colombian freight operator Aerosol (Aerovias Sol de Colombia) operates from both Bogota and Villavicencio. Douglas DC-6B HK-1700 (c/n 44419) is seen at the latter location in September 1997. Operations were suspended by the airline during 1999.

Above left: Lima, Peru-based **Aviandina** is a subsidiary of Aero Continente and has a fleet of just two aircraft. OB-1570P, an original short-bodied Boeing 727-22 (c/n 191153) is seen at base in October 2003.

Above right: **Aerogal** (Aerolineas Galapagos SA) is an Ecuadorean passenger carrier with services from its Quito base. Fairchild F-27F HC-BSL (c/n 56) is pictured at base in September 1997.

Left: Operating an international flight to Guayaquil in Ecuador in September 1997, is this **Aeroperu** Boeing 727-22 OB-1548 (c/n 19152). The Lima-based carrier suspended services in March 1999.

Above left: With a name like **Air Nostalgia**, this Australian carrier could operate one type of aircraft, the evergreen DC-3. It offers charter flights from its Melbourne-Essendon base. Douglas DC-3 VH-TMQ (c/n 32884) is photographed at base in February 2003.

Above right: With a fleet of fifteen aeroplanes, of nine different types, **Aero Condor** of Peru can offer between five and fifty seats on their aircraft. Antonov An-24RV OB-1650 (c/n 37308802) taxies to take-off at its Lima base in October 2003.

Right: British commuter carrier **Air Southwest** is based in Plymouth and flies scheduled passenger services. DHC-8-311A Dash 8 G-WOWA (c/n 296) is seen about to depart from Manchester in April 2004.

Lima-based **Aero Continente** operated a mixed fleet from an F.28 to a 767. Boeing 727-22 OB-1546P (c/n 19150) is seen at base in October 2003. Midway through 2004, following an insurance dispute, the carrier was sold to its staff and intends to restart operations as Nuevo Continente.

Above: Pictured at Moscow-Zhukovsky in August 1997, is **Air Vita Leasing Air Co** Tupolev Tu-134A-B3 RA-65693 (c/n 63221). This aircraft had a VIP interior fit. The carrier suspended operations the following year. (JDS)

Left: Based at London-Heathrow, **AFX – Air Freight Express** operated three Jumbo cargo aircraft. Boeing 747-245F G-GAFX (c/n 20827) is seen landing at base in March 2000. (SGW)

American Airlines is one of the world's largest scheduled passenger carriers. They fly both domestic and international routes. Fokker 100 N1465K (c/n 11491) is seen on one of the former at Minneapolis-St Paul in May 2000.

This **American Airlines** Boeing 777-223 N773AN (c/n 29583) was photographed on approach to London-Heathrow at the end of an Atlantic crossing in July 1999.

American Eagle flies the feeder services for American Airlines. ATR 42-300 N141DD (c/n 015) is pictured at San Juan, Puerto Rico in November 1992.

Seen at picturesque Lake Tahoe, Nevada in September 1988, is Swearingen SA-227AC Metro III N343AE (c/n AC-554) of **American Eagle**.

Left: One of the various types used as a feederliner was **American Eagle** Shorts SD.330-100 N57DD (c/n SH3003). It is seen awaiting the next load of passengers and luggage at Albany, New York in July 1986.

Below: Russian operator **Avial Aviation Company** is an all-freight carrier. Antonov An-12BP RA-11324 (c/n 2340805) is seen at the company base, Moscow-Domodedovo in August 1997. (JDS)

Above: Founded in 1936 **Aer Lingus** flies scheduled domestic, European and transatlantic passenger services. Boeing 747-130 EI-BED (c/n 19748) is seen departing its Dublin base in June 1994. Widebody Airbus A330s have replaced the Jumbo.

Below: **Aer Lingus Commuter** operated this SAAB 340B EI-CFC (c/n 340B-255). It is pictured at Dublin in June 1994.

Air Adriatic operates a fleet of two passenger jets from Rijeka in the Republic of Croatia, a country that used to be part of Yugoslavia. McDonnell Douglas MD-82 9A-CBC (c/n 49143) is seen on approach to Stansted in August 2003.

Above: Flying the Boeing 717 is **AeBal** (Aerolineas de Baleares) of Palma, Majorca. It flies as a 'Spanair Link' company. Boeing 717-2CM EC-HOA (c/n 55061) is seen landing at base in September 2000.

Left: **Avianova** ATR 72-212 EI-CLD (c/n 432) is pictured at Geneva in May 1997. This company is owned by Alitalia and flies the airline's feeder services under the name Alitalia Team. (JDS)

Above: Atlantic Airlines, part of the Air Atlantique group of companies, flies a variety of types for a number of different roles. Douglas DC-6A G-APSA (c/n 45497) with 'Atlantic Cargo' titles lands at Fairford in July 1998.

Below: Biggest and fastest of the **Atlantic Airlines** fleet is the Electra freighter. Seen showing off its elegant lines at an airshow at its Coventry base in August 2000, is Lockheed L-188CF Electra G-LOFB (c/n 1131).

Douglas DC-3 Dakota G-AMSV (c/n 32820) carries the title 'Pollution Control'. This **Atlantic Airlines** aircraft is one of a number configured to spray dispersant on any oil spills around the British coast. It is under contract from the government Maritime and Coastal Agency. It is pictured on take-off at its Coventry base in August 2000.

Convair CV-440 CS-TML (c/n 484) is owned by Atlantic Airways but has reverted to operating in the titles of **Agroar Cargo,** the Portuguese freight carrier who supplied them the craft. Photographed at Coventry in August 2000.

Right: Air Charter International was a wholly owned subsidiary of Air France. Its task was to fly charter and inclusive holiday traffic. Sud Aviation SE-210 Caravelle III F-BJTH (c/n 124) is seen at Paris-Orly in June 1971. (SGW)

Below: During the early 1980s the 'International' was dropped from the name and a new livery adopted. **Air Charter** Boeing 737-222 F-GCJL (c/n 19067) is seen arriving at Athens in June 1993. Services ceased during 1998 and aircraft were absorbed back into the Air France fleet.

Azza Air Transport of Khartoum, Sudan is an all-freight carrier. They have a fleet mix of seven aircraft of six different types. Boeing 707-330C ST-AKW (c/n 20123) is seen arriving at Sharjah, UAE in March 2000.

Above left: Alaskan freight and air taxi operator **Arctic Circle Air Service** has a number of base locations around the largest state in the union. Shorts SC.7 Skyvan 3 -200 N101WA (c/n SH1859) is seen at Fairbanks in May 2000.

Above right: **Aerovuelos** was a Colombian air taxi and commuter carrier. LET L-410UVP-E HK-4002 (c/n 861810) is pictured at the airline's Bogota base in September 1997. Operations were suspended in 1999.

Left: French regional carrier **Air Littoral** was once owned by the parent company of Swissair. From their base at Montpellier they flew both domestic and international routes. Canadair Regional Jet 100ER F-GPYR (c/n 7164) shows the airline's striking livery at Lyon in May 1997. In February 2004 services were suspended. (JDS)

Above left: Once a Portuguese colony, Macau became a semi-autonomous territory of China in December 1999. **Air Macau** is the main carrier and operates three narrow-body Airbus designs. A320-232 B-MAH (c/n 805) is seen at base in February 2003.

Above right: The nation's flag carrier, **Air Mauritius**, operates a fleet ranging from four-seat JetRangers to 294-seat Airbus wide-bodies. Airbus A340-313 3B-NAY (c/n 152) is seen departing Singapore-Changi in February 2003.

Right: Based at Sharjah, UAE, **Air Cess** registered its fleet of Soviet-built cargo aircraft in Equatorial Guinea. Ilyushin IL-18V 3C-KKJ (c/n 184006903) is seen at base in March 2000. The following year the carrier was renamed Air Bas.

Aerolineas Argentinas is the national flag carrier with services worldwide. Boeing 737-287 LV-JTO (c/n 20537) is seen on a domestic service at Buenos Aires-Aeroparque J Newbery in October 2003.

From their Winnipeg base **Air Manitoba** flew both passenger and cargo services to the many remote locations in that huge province. Curtiss C-46A Commando C-GTXW (c/n 30386) is seen at base in June 1990. Air operations were suspended in 1997.

Above: Based at Orange County, California, **Air Cal** grew following the deregulation of the American airline industry in 1979. McDonnell Douglas MD-82 N479AC (c/n 48066) is pictured at Seattle in September 1984. Three years later American Airlines bought the carrier.

Below: Based at Las Vegas, Nevada, **Allegiant Air** operates a fleet of nine McDonnell Douglas jets. Scheduled services operate between neighbouring states. Douglas DC-9-51 N401EA (c/n 47731) is seen at Long Beach in April 2000. (RO'B)

Above: African flag carrier **Air Namibia** operates short- and long-haul services from the capital Windhoek. Boeing 737-25A V5-ANA (c/n 23790) is pictured in the airline's old colours at Lusaka in April 1993. (RO'B)

Below: In the new livery of **Air Namibia** is short-body Boeing 747SP-44 ZS-SPC (c/n 21134). It is pictured on approach to London-Heathrow in July 1999.

Air Katanga is based at Kinshasa in the Democratic Republic of Congo. It flies a mixed fleet with passengers and cargo in a combi-configuration. Hawker Siddeley (BAe) Andover C1 9Q-COE (c/n Set 20) is seen at Lanseria in August 2000. The Andover was a military variant of the HS.748 built for the RAF. It had a rear-opening cargo door and a 'kneeling' undercarriage to bring the cargo ramp to floor level. (RO'B)

Dar es Salaam-based **Air Tanzania** has a small fleet of F.27 and 737 airliners. They are operated in a combi-mix of passenger and cargo services. Boeing 737-2R8C 5H-ATC (c/n 21710) is photographed on the ramp at Kampala, Uganda in November 1997. (RO'B)

Formerly a Soviet republic, Kazakstan is now an independent country. The largest airline in the new nation is **Air Kazakstan**. Tupolev Tu-134A-3 UN-65776 (c/n 62545) is seen at its Almaty base in February 1999. (RO'B)

Above left: **Australian Air Express** is an all-cargo airline based at Melbourne. Swearingen SA-227AT Expediter VH-EEN (c/n AT-563) is pictured at Brisbane-Archerfield in February 2003.

Above right: With a fleet of two aircraft, **Air Parabat** is one of two commuter airlines in Bangladesh. LET L-410UVP-E9 S2-ABM (c/n 962704) is seen on the ramp at Dhaka, its base in December 1999. (RO'B)

Left: Finally owned by Air New Zealand, **Ansett Australia** had an all-jet fleet with types ranging from an F.28 to a 747. Pictured about to depart Melbourne-Tullamarine in November 1996 is Airbus A320-211 VH-HYI (c/n 140). Operations ceased in September 2001, restarted, then finally closed down in March 2002. (RO'B)

Based on the South Pacific island of Tahiti, a French overseas territory, is **Air Tahiti Nui**. They operate a fleet of widebody Airbus designs on a growing network of destinations. A340-211 F-OITN (c/n 031) is seen arriving at Los Angeles-LAX in October 2001.

Armenian Airlines is the national airline of the former Soviet republic. Pictured on the ramp at Sharjah, UAE in March 2000, is Ilyushin IL-86 EK-86118 (c/n 51483209086). Like many airlines that have emerged from the break-up of the Soviet Union, Armenian has a truly spectacular colour scheme.

Based in Kiev, Ukraine, **ATI Aircompany** operates a fleet of nine IL-76 freighters. Pictured at Sharjah, UAE in March 2000, is Ilyushin IL-76MD UR-76629 (c/n 0053458745)

Pictured at Red Deer in May 2000, is Canadair CL-215 C-GFSM (c/n 1098). This purpose-built water bomber is operated by the government of the **Province of Alberta** to contain forest fires within its boundaries.

Above left: Honolulu-based **Aloha Airlines** operates just one type in their fleet of twenty-one: the 737. Boeing 737-2Q9 N809AL (c/n 21720) is seen at Abbotsford, British Columbia in May 2000, undergoing maintenance.

Above right: **Alpi Eagles** is an Italian regional passenger airline based at Venice, with an all Fokker fleet. Pictured approaching to land at Madrid in September 2002, is Fokker 100 I-ALPQ (c/n 11256).

Left: **ACE – Alaskan Central Express** is an all-freight carrier based at Anchorage. Beech 1900C-1 N5632C (c/n UC-81) has its two PT6 turboprops turning as it departs base in May 2000.

The Republic of Albania is the forgotten country of Europe and so has a very limited air service. Seen at Frankfurt in June 2001 is Tupolev Tu-134B-3 LZ-TUT (c/n 63987) of **Albanian Airlines**. This aircraft had been leased from Hemus Air of Bulgaria, hence the registration.

As its name implies **Alaska Air Taxi** operates services as and when required. Four of the fleet of single-engined aircraft fly on floats or wheels. The sole twin-engined aircraft is Piper PA-31 Navajo N9032Y (c/n 31-514). It is seen at the carrier's Anchorage base in May 2000.

Above left: Alitalia Express is the commuter arm of the main carrier. It operates aircraft up to 72-seat capacity.Embraer RJ145LR I-EXMB (c/n 145330) is seen at Zürich in September 2004.

Above right: The newest aircraft design to be found in the fleet of Alitalia Express is the Embraer 170LR. EI-DFG (c/n 170-00008) is pictured departing from Naples on a domestic flight in September 2004.

Left: Australian commuter line Aero Pelican Air Services is based at Newcastle, New South Wales. The fleet consists of four Twin Otters. Pictured at Sydney in September 2000, is de Havilland Canada DHC-6 Twin Otter 320 VH-KZQ (c/n 759). (RO'B)

Right: With a single aircraft, Air Vanuatu operates regional international services from its Pacific island location. Boeing 737-3Q8 YJ-AV18 (c/n 28054) is seen at Sydney, Australia in September 2000. (RO'B)

Below left: The islands of St Pierre and Miquelon are French possessions off the coast of Canada. ATR 42-320 F-OHGL (c/n 232) of Air Saint-Pierre is seen at Montreal in September 2000. (RO'B)

Below right: Wearing a very smart livery is Boeing 737-291 LV-ZYJ (c/n 22744) of Argentine scheduled passenger carrier American Falcon. It is seen at the carrier's base, Buenos Aires-Aeroparque J Newbery in October 2003.

Left: Canadian floatplane operator **Baxter Aviation** is based at Nanaimo on Vancouver Island. Services are flown to Vancouver harbour where de Havilland Canada DHC-2 Beaver 1 C-FWAC (c/n 1356) was photographed in May 2000.

Below left: Seen on take-off from Palma, Majorca in September 2000, is **British World** BAC One-Eleven 518FG G-OBWA (c/n 232). The Southend-based carrier specialised in wet-lease and sub-charter passenger operations. Operations were terminated in December 2001.

Below right: **BWIA – West Indies Airways** flies scheduled passenger services both long- and short-haul from its Port of Spain base. McDonnell Douglas MD-83 9Y-THX (c/n 49789) lands at Miami in October 1998, in the old colours of the carrier.

Above left: Showing off the striking new livery of **BWIA** is Lockheed L-1011 TriStar 500 9Y-TGJ (c/n 1179). It is pictured landing at London-Heathrow in June 2000, following the long flight from the West Indies. (SGW)

Above right: Once the second airline of the UK, **British Caledonian Airways** flew both long- and short-haul operations. Seen at Glasgow in October 1976, is BAC One-Eleven 518FG G-AYOP (c/n 233) operating a domestic service. The carrier was taken over by British Airways in 1988.

Right: **Britannia Airways** is owned by Thomson Travel to fly holidaymakers to worldwide locations. Boeing 767-304(ER) G-OBYI (c/n 29138) is ready to depart from Manchester in August 2003. It features the latest, but short lived, livery as the aircraft now carry 'Thomson' titles.

Britannia Airways AB is based in Stockholm, Sweden. It is a subsidiary of the UK company. Seen climbing out of Palma, Majorca in September 2000, is new-generation Boeing 737-804 SE-DZH (c/n 28227).

Seen on a sub-charter at Manchester in August 2003 is Boeing 737-3K9 PR-BRE (c/n 24213) of Brazilian carrier BRA Transportes Aereos. This São Paulo-based aircraft also has extra 'Rotatur' titles.

French regional carrier Brit Air is based at Morlaix. Scheduled passenger services are flown, both domestic and international. Canadair Regional Jet 100ER F-GRJI (c/n 7147) climbs out of Stuttgart in May 1997, in full livery. (JDS)

Above: The role of Brooks Fuel is to fly fuel to remote settlements and mining camps around the state of Alaska. Douglas DC-4 N90201 (c/n 10828) is seen at the company base, Fairbanks, in May 2000. As can be seen from its markings such operators regard corporate image as secondary to reliability.

Left: Many of Brit Air's services are flown as a franchise operation for Air France. Such services have the aircraft in a joint colour scheme. Canadair Regional Jet 100ER F-GRJA (c/n 7070) is seen at Frankfurt in June 1999.

Right: With just nine seats, Piper PA-31 Navajo Chieftain G-OBNW (c/n 31-7305118), is the largest of three aircraft in the fleet of British North West Airlines. The aeroplane is pictured at its Blackpool base in March 2004.

Balkan Bulgarian Airlines, like many eastern European carriers, have added western designs to their fleet mix. Boeing 737-3Y0 LZ-BOE (c/n 23923) lands, in the latest livery, at London-Heathrow in June 2000. (SGW)

Norwegian carrier Braathens is now owned by SAS. It flies scheduled passenger services around Europe. Boeing 737-405 LN-BRP (c/n 25303) is at Amsterdam in May 2001.

Above: Buffalo Airways of Yellowknife, North West Territories, operates a wide spectrum of services in northern Canada. Douglas DC-4 C-GCTF (c/n 27281) is configured as a water bomber to protect the vast areas of forest. It is photographed at base in May 2000.

Below: Flown as a cargo aircraft carrying all the necessities to remote locations that lack road access is Buffalo Airways Curtiss C-46D Commando C-FAVO (c/n 33242). It is seen being loaded at Yellowknife on a cold day in May 2000. Note the hot-air heater attached to the starboard engine.

Above: Paris, France-based passenger carrier Blue Line has a fleet of three aircraft. Largest is McDonnell Douglas MD-83 F-GMLI (c/n 53014). It is seen departing Manchester in April 2004 on its way to Nice.

Below: Bouraq Indonesian Airlines is based in the capital, Jakarta. With two types of airliner it flies regional international services. McDonnell Douglas MD-82 PK-IMC (c/n 49113) is seen at Singapore-Changi in February 2003.

Bahamasair is the largest airline from that island group. De Havilland Canada DHC-8 Dash 8-311 C6-BFG (c/n 288) is pictured landing at Miami following a flight from Nassau, the carrier's base in October 1998.

Belavia is the main passenger airline in the former Soviet republic of Belarus. Tupolev Tu-134A EW-65108 (c/n 60322) is pictured landing at London-Gatwick in August 1997.

Left: At one time the best way to transport a car and passengers across the English Channel to France was by air. Bristol 170 Mk.32 Superfreighter G-APAU (c/n 13256) of **British Air Ferries** is seen being loaded with a car at its Lydd base in July 1970. Faster ships and hovercraft led to the rundown of this flying service.

Below: **bmi – British Midland Airways** flies scheduled passenger services for both domestic, European and North American operations. Airbus A330-243 G-WWBB (c/n 404) is pictured departing on one of the latter, at Manchester in June 2002.

British Air Ferries went on to provide passenger charter and cargo services. BAC One-Eleven 416EK G-SURE (c/n 129) is seen at Manchester in October 1982. The carrier was renamed British World in April 1993.

bmi Regional is the commuter arm of British Midland. It has an all-jet fleet. Embraer RJ135ER G-RJXJ (c/n 145473) is seen at Manchester in August 2003.

Above: **bmi Baby** is the low-cost arm of British Midland. They have aircraft based at several UK airports. Boeing 737-37Q G-ODSK (c/n 28537) is seen at Manchester in August 2003.

Right: **British Island Airways** operated domestic passenger services in the UK including the Isle of Man and the Channel Islands. BAC One-Eleven 513FS G-AYWB (c/n 237) is seen at Manchester in April 1987. Operations were suspended in 1990.

Airbus A310-325 HB-IPL (c/n 640) of Balair/CTA shows the markings of the joint company; note the yellow wings. It is pictured landing at Zürich in August 1998.

Above: Owned by Swissair, Balair flew holiday charter operations. Airbus A310-322 HB-IPK (c/n 412) is seen at its Zürich base in August 1987. The company was merged with CTA to form Balair/CTA and was later absorbed into the parent company. It was then relaunched as Balair again.

Right: Dallas-based Braniff was one of the early casualties of the 1979 airline deregulation. Douglas DC-8-62 N1804 (c/n 45896) lands at Miami in October 1981, in a green colour scheme. This livery style was applied a number of different colours. The carrier suspended operations in the early part of 1982.

In 1984 Braniff was reborn with a new livery. Boeing 727-227 N457BN (c/n 21463) is pictured at Washington-National in May 1989. In November of that year services ceased operating for the final time.

Above: This British Airways/Cambrian BAC One-Eleven 408EF G-AVGP (c/n 114) is seen at Palma, Majorca in November 1974. Cambrian, a UK independent, was originally formed in 1935, and became a totally-owned part of British Air Service in 1967. By 1972 it was a regional division of BA and was absorbed into the main unit.

Left: Pictured at Palma, Majorca in November 1973, is Hawker Siddeley HS.121 Trident 1E-140 G-AVYB (c/n 2136) in the mixed colours of British Airways/Northeast. The name Northeast had come about in November 1970 when UK independent BKS changed its name to reflect the region it served. In 1973, via their parent company, they became part of BA: hence the hybrid scheme.

Pictured at Shetland airport in December 1975 is Sikorsky S-58ET G-BCLN (c/n 581539) of **British Airways Helicopters**. One of the main services flown was to support the North Sea oil industry. The name was changed to British International Helicopters in 1986. (RO'B)

British Airtours was the holiday charter arm of British Airways. Lockheed L-1011 TriStar 1 G-BBAJ (c/n 1106) is seen at London-Gatwick in July 1987. The carrier was renamed Caledonian following the 1988 takeover by BA of British Caledonian.

Left: British European became the new operating name for Jersey European. The change, from June 2000, reflected the wider range of routes flown. BAe 146-200 G-JEAY (c/n E2138) is pictured landing at London-Heathrow in July 2002. The carrier has since adopted the new name of Flybe.

Right: Bangkok Airways is a Thai regional carrier operating both domestic and local international services. Boeing 717-23S HS-PGP (c/n 55064) is seen at its Bangkok base in January 2002.

Below: CASA 212-200 N117BH (c/n 171) of **Bighorn Airways** is seen being operated by the Bureau of Land Management at Fort Wainwright, Alaska in May 2000. The type is the biggest aircraft in the Sheridan, Wyoming carrier's mixed fleet.

Nigerian carrier **Bellview Airlines** operated a twice-weekly scheduled service from its Lagos base to Amsterdam-Schiphol. Airbus A300-622R 5N-BVU (c/n 633) is pictured at the latter location in October 1999.

Based at London-Gatwick, **BAC Express Airlines** flies cargo F.27 and Shorts 360s in a combi role on freight and passenger services. Shorts SD.360-300 G-VBAC (c/n SH3736) is seen at Fairford in July 1999 on a charter.

Above: **BH Air** is a Sofia-based holiday charter airline. Airbus A320-211 LZ-BHA (c/n 029) is seen at Manchester in August 2004.

Left: The four Tupolev Tu-154Ms of BH Air just carry the titles **Balkan Holiday Airlines**. They look very stylish in their multicoloured livery. LZ-HMI (c/n 706) is pictured about to depart from Manchester in June 2002.

Seen at New York's state capital Albany in July 1986, is **Business Express** Beech 1900C N809BE (c/n UB-40). The carrier provided feeder services for a number of the major US airlines.

Brasmex – Brasil Minas Express operated from 2001 to 2004 with a single McDonnell Douglas DC-10-30F. PR-BME (c/n 47819) is pictured, in April 2004, at São Paulo-Guarulhos. (RO'B)

Buzz was set up as a low-cost carrier by KLM for operations based in the UK. BAe 146-300 G-UKID (c/n E3157) is seen at Frankfurt in June 2001. The airline has been bought by Ryanair and absorbed into its new parent.

French carrier **Belair** operated a pair of MD-83s and 727s. Boeing 727-227 F-GCGQ (c/n 20609) is at Paris-CDG in June 1997. Services by the Orly-based carrier were suspended in January 2000. (JDS)

Above left: Finnish carrier **Blue 1** used to known as Air Botnia; it is now part of the SAS group. BAe 146 RJ85 OH-SAO (c/n E2393) is seen departing Berlin-Tegel in May 2004.

Above right: **BCM Airlines** was a Palma-based Spanish charter airline. Airbus A320-231 EC-GLT (c/n 314) is seen at Frankfurt in June 1997. The company ceased operations the following January.

Right: National flag carrier **Biman Bangladesh Airlines** flies both long- and short-haul operations. BAe ATP S2-ACY (c/n 2027) is seen at Blackpool in March 2004 following its sale to a UK operator.

Above left: Canadian carrier **Bearskin Airlines** flies commuter services around the north of Ontario and surrounding provinces. Piper PA-31 T3-1040 C-FYPL (c/n 31T-3275014) is seen on a charter at Pickle Lake in June 1990.

Above right: **Bulgarian Air Charter** has a fleet of five 166-seat Russian-built Tupolev airliners. Tu-154M LZ-LCV (c/n 733) is pictured at Berlin-Tegel in May 2004.

Right: The DHA-3 Drover was made famous by its operations for the Royal Flying Doctor Service in Australia. VH-ADN (c/n 5009) is now operated by **Bathurst Vintage Joy Flights** from Bathurst in New South Wales. It is pictured at base in February 2003.

Right: Cebu Pacific Air is a Manila-based low-cost operator flying both domestic and regional international passenger services. Boeing 757-236 RP-C2715 (c/n 24371) is seen at Hong Kong in March 2003.

Below left: Once one of the great names of Canadian transport, CP Air, formerly Canadian Pacific, merged with Pacific Western in 1987 to form Canadian. McDonnell Douglas DC-10-30 C-GCPJ (c/n 46991) is seen at Toronto in July 1986.

Above right: Photographed at Johannesburg in July 2001, is Cameroon Airlines Boeing 737-33A TJ-CBH (c/n 27457). The airline operates domestic and African services as well as scheduled flights to the principal European capitals from its base at Douala. (RO'B)

Left: Cirrus Airways of Saarbrücken flies scheduled European commuter services. They are a Lufthansa Partner and some of their services are code-shares. De Havilland Canada DHC-8-314 Dash 8 Series 300 D-BKIM (c/n 356) is seen at Zürich in September 2004.

Below left: Dublin-based CityJet flew services under a franchise agreement with Virgin. BAe 146-100 EI-CJP (c/n E1160) lands at base in June 1994. The airline is now a subsidiary of Air France.

Above right: Reflecting the ownership of CityJet by Air France, most of the carrier's aircraft now fly in the parent company's livery with CityJet titles. BAe 146-300 EI-DEV (c/n E3123) is pictured at Zürich in September 2004.

Left: Champion Air is an American 727 operator with a fleet of eighteen aircraft. Boeing 727-257 N684CA (c/n 22491) is seen at the airline's Minneapolis-St Paul base in May 2000.

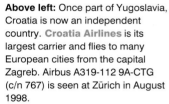

Greek charter carrier **Cronus Airlines** was formed in 1995 and has an all-737 fleet of seven aircraft. Boeing 737-4Y0 SX-BGH (c/n 23866) is seen at Frankfurt in June 1999.

Above left: Once part of Yugoslavia, Croatia is now an independent country. **Croatia Airlines** is its largest carrier and flies to many European cities from the capital Zagreb. Airbus A319-112 9A-CTG (c/n 767) is seen at Zürich in August 1998.

Right: Airbus A330-202 C-GGWC (c/n 272) of Toronto-based **Canada 3000** is pictured on approach to Manchester in June 2000. This charter operator has aircraft in size from the A320 to a 340-seat A330.

Condor is the largest holiday charter line in Germany, an all-Boeing operator and a subsidiary of Lufthansa. Boeing 757-330 D-ABOE (c/n 29012) is seen approaching the gate at the carrier's Frankfurt base in June 1999. This airline was the launch customer for the stretched '300' series 757.

Above: As with the USSR and Aeroflot, all Chinese civil airliners were once operated by **CAAC** (Civil Aviation Administration of China). Seen at Bangkok in November 1989, is Boeing 757-21B B-2804 (c/n 24330).

Below: Long-haul flights from China to Europe by **CAAC** used 747s. Pictured at London-Gatwick in July 1987, is N1301E a short-body, long-range Boeing 747SP-27 (c/n 22302). During the latter part of this decade the government in China allowed the regions to run their own airlines.

Condor Berlin is a subsidiary of Condor and has an all-Airbus fleet. Airbus A320-212 D-AICE (c/n 894) is pictured at Frankfurt in June 1999.

Cygnus Air is a Spanish cargo operator with a fleet of three. Douglas DC-8-62F EC-EMD (c/n 46023) is pictured landing at the carrier's base, Madrid, in September 2002.

Based in Gothenburg, **City Airline** is a Swedish regional commuter carrier with a fleet of three aircraft. Embraer RJ145LR SE-RAC (c/n 145098) is seen lined up to depart from Manchester's Runway 24L in August 2002.

Right: Seen at a sunlit but wet Amsterdam in August 1997, is **City Hopper** Fokker 70 PH-KZI (c/n 11579). The airline now flies as KLM Cityhopper in virtually full KLM livery.

Below: China Northern Airlines of Shenyang operates a complete mix of aircraft, with roles ranging from agricultural spraying to air transport services. Largest aircraft in the fleet is the Airbus A300B4-622R. B-2329 (c/n 762) is seen on touchdown at Guangzhou in October 1999.
The carrier is being merged into China Southern Airlines.

Above: Hong Kong airline **Cathay Pacific** only operates long-range, large aircraft. The smallest is the twin-aisle and twin-engine A330. Seen landing at Zürich in August 1998, is Airbus A340-313 B-HXK (c/n 228).

Below: The A330 and 777 are direct competitors, **Cathay Pacific** operates both. Boeing 777-367 B-HNK (c/n 27510) is seen at Bangkok in November 1999. The '300' series 777 is the stretched variant.

China Yunnan Airlines have an all-Boeing fleet of 737s. From its base at Kunming it flies both domestic and international services. B-2502 (c/n 30075) is a new-generation Boeing 737-7WO. It is seen landing at Guangzhou in October 1999. Note the taller fin of this variant. The airline is being merged into China Eastern Airlines.

Flying the freight for the group is **Cathay Pacific Cargo**. Boeing 747-267F B-HVZ (c/n 23864) lands at Frankfurt in June 1999.

Central Air Service is an Arizona-based water-bomber operator. The DC-4 fleet is available to provide fire protection to forest areas. Douglas DC-4 N96451 (c/n 10592) is pictured at Tucson in September 1988.

Seen departing Quito, Ecuador in September 1997, is Tupolev Tu-154M CU-T1265 (c/n 751) of **Cubana**. From the airline's Havana base it flies services to South and Central America as well as Canada.

Above left: Venezuelan commuter line **Cave** (Compania Aerea de Viajes Expressos) operated between 1987 and 1993. Britten-Norman BN2A Mk.111 Trislander YV-488C (c/n 1012) is seen at Caracas in November 1992.

Right: The Xian Y-7 is a Chinese-built Antonov An-24. The '200' series Y-7 has Pratt & Whitney (Canada) PW150A turboprops for better performance and economy. Xian Y-7-200A B-3720 (c/n 0001) of local carrier **Changan Air** is seen at the company base of Xian in October 1999. This carrier is now part of the Hainan Airlines group.

Below left: **Cyprus Airways** are an all-Airbus airline with A330, A320 and A319 designs. Services are flown from the Mediterranean island to all points of the compass. Airbus A320-231 5B-DAV (c/n 037) is seen at Frankfurt in June 1999.

Charter America is a charter and brokerage company. They have a number of Custom Air Transport 727 freighters in its livery. Boeing 727-291F N406BN (c/n 19991) is seen at Minneapolis-St Paul in May 2000.

Russian passenger carrier **Chernomorskie Airlines** has been renamed Chernomor Avia. Tupolev Tu-134A RA-65575 (c/n 62350) is at Sharjah, UAE in March 2000, a long way from the airline's Sochi base.

Above: Passenger airline **Chelyabinsk Air Enterprise** is based in the Russian city of that name. Pictured at Moscow-Domodedovo in August 1997, is Tupolev Tu-154B-2 RA-85467 (c/n 467). (JDS)

Below: **Carter Air Services**, of Hay River, North West Territories, have just one large aircraft. Cessna 208 Caravan 1 C-GJEM (c/n 208-00152) is photographed at base in May 2000. This aircraft can operate as an amphibian, able to use the many lakes in the region. Both passengers and freight are carried.

Above: **Conifair** was a Canadian water-bombing and insect-spraying company.Douglas DC-6/C-118 C-GBYA (c/n 43717) is seen at the company base of St Jean, Quebec in July 1986. In 1997 the company ceased flying operations and now provides maintenance services.

Below: Swiss regional carrier **Crossair** had a large fleet and European route network. McDonnell Douglas MD-83 HB-ISX (c/n 49844) shows off the airline's then latest livery at Palma, Majorca in September 2000. Following the demise of Swissair, Crossair took over the flag-carrier's network and renamed itself Swiss.

Associated with Luxair, **Cargolux Airlines International** is a major freight carrier with a fleet of thirteen Jumbos. Boeing 747-4R7F LX-FCV (c/n 25866) is pictured making a sharp turn to land on Runway 32 at Zürich in August 1998.

Seen on the runway at Seattle-Tacoma in September 1984, is Avro (Hawker Siddeley) 748 Srs.2B N118CA (c/n 1789) of regional passenger carrier **Cascade Airways**. The following year services were suspended.

Right: De Havilland DH.104 Dove VH-ABM (c/n 04097) of **Central Australian Airways** is seen at Melbourne-Essendon in November 1975. (RO'B)

Below: South African regional carrier **Comair** Fokker F.27 Friendship ZS-KVJ (c/n 10264) is pictured at Gaborone, Botswana in March 1992, in the company livery. The airline now has a franchise agreement with British Airways and flies in that company's colours. (RO'B)

Above: **Cypress Airlines** of Vancouver had three Convairs. Operations were started in June 1996 and ceased the following year. Convair CV-580 C-GTTG (c/n 508) is seen in store at Kelowna, British Columbia in May 2000.

Below: UK independent **Classic Airways** had a short life. Founded in 1997 they ceased operations in August of the following year. Lockheed L-1011 TriStar 100 G-IOII (c/n 1118) is seen in store at Stansted in August 1999.

Above: Another **Comair**, this one is a major American commuter carrier owned by Delta. The livery is a variant of the parent company's and has Delta Connection on the cabin roof and Comair on the tail. Canadair Regional Jet 100ER N971CA (c/n 7145) is seen on approach to Miami in October 1998.

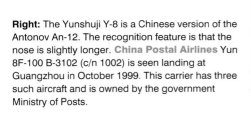

Right: The Yunshuji Y-8 is a Chinese version of the Antonov An-12. The recognition feature is that the nose is slightly longer. **China Postal Airlines** Yun 8F-100 B-3102 (c/n 1002) is seen landing at Guangzhou in October 1999. This carrier has three such aircraft and is owned by the government Ministry of Posts.

Carga Aero Transportada was a Bolivian meat carrier. This task involves flying freshly killed cattle from the lowland farms to the capital La Paz (12,000 feet above sea level). Convair CV-340 CP-2026 (c/n 249) is seen at La Paz in November 1992. The airline ceased operations in 1994.

Above: The Cayman Islands is a well-known offshore banking centre. Based in the capital, Georgetown, on Grand Cayman is Cayman Airways. Boeing 727-227 N271AF (c/n 22003) is seen landing at Miami in June 1989.

Below: CDF Aviation (California Department of Forestry) operates a small fleet of water bombers and their support aircraft. Grumman S-2A Tracker N450DF (c/n 421) is seen at Santa Rosa in September 1988.

Above: Copa Airlines is the largest carrier in the Central American republic of Panama. They have an affiliation with US airline Continental; this is reflected in their livery. Boeing 737-7V3 HP-1377CMP (c/n 30642) is seen at Lima, Peru in October 2003. The winglets on this new-generation 737 are very apparent.

Below: One of Canada's largest water-bomber operators is Conair of Abbotsford, British Columbia. Douglas DC-6B C-GHCA (c/n 45197) is pictured at base in September 1984.

Above: Corsair is a Paris Orly-based holiday charter company. They fly both long- and short-haul trips. Boeing 747-128 F-BPVG (c/n 20377) is seen on approach to London-Heathrow in July 1999.

Right: Challenge Air Cargo has been one of the leading freight airlines at Miami for over fifteen years. McDonnell Douglas DC-10-40F N157DM (c/n 46920) is seen at base in October 1998. The company was renamed Centurion Air Cargo in August 2001.

Birmingham-based **Community Express Airlines** was a small commuter line. Shorts 360 G-OBOH (c/n SH3713) is at Liverpool on a scheduled service in June 1996. Services were suspended three months later.

An all-cargo carrier, **Channel Express** is one of the leading freight airlines in the UK. Airbus A300B4-203F G-CEXH (c/n 117) is seen on a service to Sharjah, UAE in March 2000.

Norwegian regional operator **Color Air** operated three UK-registered 737s. Pictured at Stansted in August 1999, is Boeing 737-3QB G-COLB (c/n 26283) arriving on a scheduled service from Oslo. The following month the airline suspended operations.

Above: **Chalk's Ocean Airways** has a history dating back to 1919, making them one of the world's oldest carriers. Grumman G-73 Turbo Mallard N2969 (c/n J-27) enters the water at Bimini, Bahamas on route to its Miami-Watson Island seaplane base in October 1981.

Left: Operating the only airworthy Cargomaster in the world is Anchorage-based **Cargomaster Corporation**. The ex-USAF bulk transport's use is limited to federal and state contracts only. Douglas C-133A Cargomaster N199AB (c/n 45164) is seen at base in May 2000.

Seen on take-off from Lanzhou in October 1999, is Yunshuji Y-5 B-8238 (c/n 316409) of **China Northwest Airlines**. The Yun 5 is a Chinese-built Antonov An-2. Note the local modification of the wingtips. This is to improve airflow for crop-spraying operations.

China Northwest Airlines BAe 146-300 B-2718 (c/n E3222) is on the ramp at Lanzhou in October 1999, preparing for a morning domestic service. The passenger fleet of the carrier included Airbus A300, A310 and A320 aircraft. The company has since been absorbed into China Eastern Airlines.

Based at Shanghai, **China Eastern Airlines** operates a wide range of both American and European designs. McDonnell Douglas MD-90-30 B-2256 (c/n 53582) touches down at Guangzhou in October 1999.

Above: Established in 1989, **China General Aviation** operated a number of types. As well as general aviation operations they flew some schedules and charters. Yakovlev Yak-42D B-2754 (c/n 4520423116579) is seen arriving at Guangzhou in October 1999. At the start of 1998 the airline had been taken over by China Eastern, which had not yet repainted their new aircraft.

Right: Airbus A320-214 B-2209 (c/n 1030) of China Eastern Airlines arrives at the gate at Beijing in October 1999. This is one of fifty-seven A320s on the company fleet list or on order.

Below: **CNAC – Zhejiang Airlines** Airbus A320-214 B-2376 (c/n 876) is seen at Beijing in October 1999. This carrier, based at Hangzhou, operates Dash 8 commuters as well as the Airbus. The company was merged into Air China in 2004.

Above: Founded in 1987 in Chengdu, **China Southwest Airlines** operate a fleet of 737s and 757s together with three widebody four-engine Airbus aircraft. Airbus A340-313 B-2388 (c/n 242) is seen at Guangzhou in October 1999. The airline is soon to be absorbed into Air China.

Below: In warm evening sunlight, **China Southwest Airlines** Boeing 737-3Z0 B-2950 (c/n 27374) arrives at Beijing in October 1999.

Founded in 1992 by the Beijing Municipal Government, **China Xinhua Airlines** operates domestic services with an all-Boeing fleet. Boeing 737-341 B-2908 (c/n 26854) is seen on a service to Guangzhou in October 1999. This company is now part of the Hainan Airlines group.

China Southern Airlines operates services to such distant locations as California. Boeing 777-21B B-2051 (c/n 27357) is seen on the runway at the carrier's Guangzhou base in October 1999.

Above: The Xinjiang province of China is an autonomous region in the far west of the country. China Xinjiang Airlines, the carrier for the region, is now part of the China Southern group. Boeing 757-28C B-2859 (c/n 29217) it seen at its Urumqi base in October 1999.

Left: One of the last Chinese airlines to have operated Russian-built aircraft, China Xinjiang Airlines Tupolev Tu-154M B-2603 (c/n 718) retracts its wheels at Urumqi in October 1999.

Only one carrier in China operated the Ilyushin IL-86 Russian widebody. China Xinjiang Airlines Ilyushin IL-86 B-2016 (c/n 51483210097) is seen at Beijing in October 1999.

Above: China Airlines is one of the main carriers in the Republic of China (Taiwan). Services are flown worldwide. Airbus A300B4-622R B-18571 (c/n 529) arrives at its gate at Bangkok in November 1999.

Below: Pictured at Anchorage in May 2000, is this leased Boeing 747-47UF N497MC (c/n 29258). It is in the full livery of China Airlines Cargo. Note that the cargo variant of the 747-400 does not have the stretched upper deck of the passenger carriers.

The ATR 72 commuter airliner is only flown by one Chinese (People's Republic) airline. Pictured at Urumqi in October 1999, is ATR 72-500 B-3027 (c/n 555) of China Xinjiang Airlines.

Pictured at Bangkok in November 1989 is Ilyushin IL-62 OK-GBH (c/n 62404) in the old livery of **CSA-Czechoslovak Airlines**. This was prior to the peaceful split with the Slovak Republic.

CSA-Czech Airlines, like so many former eastern bloc countries, have replaced their Russian aircraft with western types. Airbus A310-304 OK-WAB (c/n 567) is seen at Bangkok in November 1999.

CSA-Czech Airlines operate a number of commuter airliners. ATR 72-202 OK-XFC (c/n 299) is seen at Amsterdam-Schiphol in August 1997.

This Tupolev Tu-134A OK-EFK (c/n 4323130) shows the new livery of **CSA** at London-Heathrow in June 1992. These Soviet-built gas-guzzlers have been withdrawn, this particular aircraft in 1995.

Houston-based **Continental Airlines** is one of the major carriers in America. Services both domestic and international are flown. N601PE Boeing 747-238B (c/n 20535) is pictured in the red-ball tail logo livery at Los Angeles-LAX in September 1988.

Many commuter airlines are looking towards an all-jet fleet. The Brazilian Embraer RJ145LR is one of the best-selling aircraft in this field. N14952 (c/n 145067) of **Continental Express** is seen at Minneapolis-St Paul in May 2000.

Showing the new livery introduced in 1993 by **Continental Airlines** is Boeing 737-3TO N14342 (c/n 23580). It is seen at its gate at Minneapolis-St Paul in May 2000.

Right: Canadian was one of the two main passenger carriers in Canada. Boeing 767-375 C-FCAJ (c/n 24086) is pictured at Winnipeg, Manitoba in June 1990. At the start of the year 2000, Air Canada began their takeover.

Below: Showing off the new Canadian livery, that was to be short-lived, is Boeing 747-475 C-FCRA (c/n 24895). It is seen at Bangkok in November 1999 and shows the goose emblem on the fin.

Above: Canadian North have a fleet of two 737s for passenger operations in the far north. Canadian operates its flights with revised titles. Boeing 737-275C C-GOPW (c/n 22160) is seen at the carrier's Yellowknife base in May 2000. This aircraft is a combi with freight in the front; note the cargo door is open, and passengers to the rear.

Below: The other airline type operated by Canadian Regional is the home-produced Dash 8. De Havilland Canada DHC-8 Dash 8-301 C-GETA (c/n 186) is seen at Edmonton, Alberta in May 2000.

Above: Canadian Partner provides commuter and feeder services for the parent company; the similar livery reflects this. Embraer EMB-120RT Brasilia C-GDOE (c/n 120178) is pictured on the move at Hamilton, Ontario in June 1990.

Right: Canadian Regional flies scheduled commuter services. Fokker F.28 Fellowship 1000 C-GTEO (c/n 11991) arrives at Kelowna, British Columbia in May 2000.

Right: DutchBird was an Amsterdam-based passenger carrier with a Boeing and Airbus fleet mix. Boeing 757-230 PH-DBH (c/n 24748) is seen at base in May 2001.

Below: Ukraine airline Dniprovia operates passenger services with Yak-40s or -42s. Pictured at Moscow-Vnukovo in August 1997, is UR-87841 Yakovlev Yak-40 (c/n 9330930). This tri-jet is configured with thirty seats. (JDS)

Above: Delta Air Lines of Atlanta is one of the largest American scheduled passenger carriers. McDonnell Douglas MD-90-30 N913DN (c/n 53393) is seen in the traditional livery on a domestic flight at Phoenix, Arizona in October 1999.

Below: A further revision of the Delta Air Lines colour scheme was introduced in March 2000. It is to be seen on this Boeing 767-432(ER) N833MH (c/n 29706), pictured landing at Los Angles-LAX in October 2001. The '400' series of the 767 is the longest of the three versions.

Above: Pictured landing at London-Gatwick in August 1997, is McDonnell Douglas MD-11 N809DE (c/n 48480) of Delta Air Lines. It is arriving at the end of a transatlantic service.

Below: Delta Air Lines revised its livery in 1997 as can be seen with this Boeing 727-232 N522DA (c/n 21582). It is pictured at Minneapolis-St Paul in May 2000.

Hong Kong-based **Dragonair** flies an all-Airbus fleet of A320, A321 and A330 aircraft for its passenger services. Pictured at Beijing in October 1999 is Airbus A330-342 B-HYD (c/n 132).

Above: Druk Air is the sole commercial airline in the Kingdom of Bhutan. BAe 146-100 A5-RGE (c/n E1199) is seen departing Bangkok in November 1999, for its return flight to Paro in the Himalayan kingdom.

Right: British independent **Dan Air** operated Comets for fourteen years. A total of 32 were put into service, with many more bought just for spares. De Havilland DH.106 Comet 4 G-APYC (c/n 6437) climbs out of Palma, Majorca in November 1973. The carrier was taken over by British Airways in 1992.

Above left: Dan Air operated a single Nord 262A-22 in its search for a Dakota replacement. It was operated for eighteen months before being supplanted by HS.748s. G-AYFR (c/n 29) is at Liverpool-Speke in May 1971.

Above right: Based at Sydney-Bankstown, **Dakota National Air** has seven passenger-configured DC-3s. Douglas DC-3 VH-SBL (c/n 12056) is seen at base in April 2000. (RO'B)

Left: Denim Air is a Dutch scheduled passenger carrier based at Eindhoven. Fokker 50 PH-DMS (c/n 20209) is photographed at Zürich in September 2004.

On lease from Air Cess to **Damal Airlines** is Ilyushin IL-18E 3C-KKR (c/n 185008603). It is seen at the Air Cess base of Sharjah, UAE in March 2000.

Above: German regional carrier **DLT** (Deutsche Luftverkehrsgesellschaft) was based at Frankfurt. De Havilland Canada DHC-8 Dash 8-311 D-BEAT (c/n 210) is seen at Farnborough, prior to delivery in September 1990. The airline was renamed Lufthansa Cityline in March 1992.

Below: Hong Kong-based **Dragonair Cargo** operates four Jumbos in an all-cargo role. Pictured on take-off at Manchester in August 2003 is Boeing 747-3H6 B-KAC (c/n 23600). This flight is a regular service.

Above: Antonov An-24RV 3C-KKH (c/n 27307701) of **Damal Airlines** is seen on the ramp at Sharjah, UAE in March 2000. The company logo is in a low-key form on the front fuselage.

Below: Russian passenger and freight operator **Don Avia** is based at Rostov-on-Don. Pictured arriving at Düsseldorf in September 1998, is Tupolev Tu-154B-2 RA-85452 (c/n 452).

Right: With a basic Ilyushin fleet of IL-62, -76 and -96 aircraft types **Domodedovo Airlines** is based at the Moscow airport of the same name. Ilyushin IL-62M RA-86501 (c/n 3933121) is seen at base in August 1995.

Below: **DAS Air Cargo** currently has an all DC-10 fleet. Regular services to the UK are flown from the carrier's Entebbe, Uganda base. Now gone from the operator, Boeing 707-369C 5X-JON (c/n 20546) is seen at London-Gatwick in August 1993.

Operating in summer months only, **Denali Air** of Alaska is based at McKinley National Park. Beech D18S Tri-gear N766L (c/n A-952) is seen at Merrill Field, Anchorage in May 2000.

Showing that the type will seemingly go on forever is Douglas DC-3 ZS-PTG (c/n 13331). Seen at Lanseria, August 2000, is a Debon Air machine with **Delaney** titles. This South African operator flies tours with its three aircraft. (RO'B)

Above: To add further lease to the life of the evergreen DC-3 many aircraft have had their piston engines removed and replaced with turboprops. One such is this **Dodson Aviation** machine. N145RD (c/n 20175) is at California City in October 2001.

Right: When owned by British Airways, Munich-based **Deutsche BA** had a European-wide network of scheduled services with a fleet of 737s. Boeing 737-31S D-ADBQ (c/n 29099) is on approach to London-Gatwick in August 1998. The controversial BA tail marks were applied to the carrier's aircraft with some dedicated German designs. This one is 'Avignon' created by Berlin artist Jim Avignon.

This **Deutsche BA** Boeing 737-3L9 D-ADBF (c/n 24571) seen at Düsseldorf, in September 1998, shows the tail marks 'Bavaria'. Herbert Reiger created these.

Boeing 737-31S D-ADBN (c/n 29058) seen at Düsseldorf in September 1998, shows the **Deutsche BA** – specific tail design 'Calligraphy'. This was created by Gottfied Pott and features old gothic script.

Above left: Now independent from British Airways, Deutsche BA is now known as **DBA**. It has revised its livery to reflect this. Boeing 737-36Q D-ADIB (c/n 30334) is seen at Berlin-Tegel in May 2004.

Above right: Seen at Lanseria, South Africa in December 1999 is Cessna 208B Caravan ZS-OAT (c/n 208B-366). Owned by Helicopter Services, it is in the livery of **DHL** for parcel transport. (RO'B)

Left: **DHL** use this Dassault Falcon 20C HC-BSS (c/n 150) for the transport of parcels in Ecuador. Pictured in its hangar, in September 1997, at Guayaquil, it is operated for DHL by Trans Am (Express del Ecuador).

Below: **DHL International** is the Middle East wing of the worldwide parcel carrier DHL. Boeing 757-23AP(F) VH-AWE (c/n 24635) is seen on approach to Dubai in March 1997.

Above: Taiwanese passenger and cargo company **EVA Air** is owned by the American Evergreen group of companies. Boeing 757-27A B-27021 (c/n 29611) is seen on a service to Macau in February 2003. This 757 is not in the EVA fleet as this aeroplane is on lease from FAT.

Ecuatoriana of Quito, Ecuador was owned by VASP of Brazil. The livery of McDonnell Douglas DC-10-30 PP-SFB (c/n 46575) reflected this. It is pictured about to depart Miami in evening sunshine in October 1998.

Below: **EVA Air Cargo** is the freight side of the company with eleven MD-11 cargo aircraft together with four 747s. McDonnell Douglas MD-11F B-16110 (c/n 48786) is seen departing the ramp at Sharjah, UAE in March 2000.

Antonov An-32 3C-5GE (c/n 1609) is owned by the government of **Equatorial Guinea**. It is operated in a rare mix of VIP and combi roles. Pictured at Sharjah, UAE in March 2000. Note the unusual mix of alphanumeric characters in the registration.

Above left: **Excel Airways** used to be known as Sabre Airways. They are a Gatwick-based holiday charter carrier with an all Boeing fleet. Seen departing Manchester in August 2002 is Boeing 737-8Q8 G-XLAA (c/n 28226).

Above right: **ERA Classic Airlines** is part of ERA and flies two DC-3s for charter and tourism work. Douglas DC-3 N1944H (c/n 34378) is at Merrill Field, Anchorage in May 2000.

Right: **Everts Air Fuel** is one of a small number of operators who specialise in the shipment of fuel oils to remote locations. Curtiss C-46F Commando N1822M (c/n 22521) named 'Salmon Ella' is seen at the carrier's Fairbanks, Alaska base in May 2000.

Exin Co is a Polish, Katowice-based freight carrier with a fleet of five Russian-built transport aircraft. Antonov An-26B SP-FDO (c/n 10503) is pictured departing Liverpool in May 2004 on a motor industry parts charter.

Above: Shannon in the west of Ireland is the home base of EUJet. The airline operates a fleet of four 104-seat Fokker aircraft. Fokker 100 EI-DFC (c/n 11296) is seen at Manchester in July 2004.

Left: Eastern Airlines was one of America's longest-running carriers with a history going back as far as 1928. Airbus A300B4-103 N219EA (c/n 120) is seen at their Miami base in October 1981. In January 1991 the airline ceased operations.

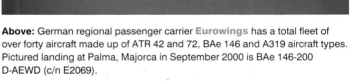

Above: German regional passenger carrier Eurowings has a total fleet of over forty aircraft made up of ATR 42 and 72, BAe 146 and A319 aircraft types. Pictured landing at Palma, Majorca in September 2000 is BAe 146-200 D-AEWD (c/n E2069).

Above: The holiday and offshore banking centre of the Isle of Man is home to Euromanx. Regular passenger services are flown, with leased Dutch aircraft, to UK mainland cities. Seen arriving at Liverpool in June 2004 is ATR 42-300 PH-RAQ (c/n 139).

Right: British operator Eastern Airways is based at Humberside. They have a growing fleet of commuter aircraft, particularly Jetstreams. Pictured at Manchester in March 2004 is BAe 4100 Jetstream 41 G-MAJF (c/n 41008).

Pictured at Minneapolis-St Paul in May 2000, is Douglas DC-8-62F N993CF (c/n 46028) of **Emery Worldwide**. This company is one of the giants of US cargo services, it has a fleet of over 80 aircraft made up of 727, DC-8 and DC-10 types.

Above: One of the fastest-growing UK low-cost operators is **easyJet**. It now has several bases from which it operates an extensive network of domestic and European destinations. Boeing 737-33V G-EZYO (c/n 29339) is seen climbing out of Palma, Majorca in September 2000. The carrier now has its website address on the aircraft replacing the telephone number of earlier years. This reflects its claim to be 'the web's favourite airline'.

Below: Geneva-based **easyJet Switzerland**, is an associate of the UK operation. Airbus A319-111 HB-JZB (c/n 2043) is seen at Liverpool in May 2004, operating a service to its home base. It is of note that, due to the number of seats in the carrier's A319s (156), they have two overwing exits – not the usual single one for this model.

Above: Estonia, the Baltic republic, has embraced western equipment with **Estonian Air**. It is associated with the Danish airline Maersk. Boeing 737-5Q8 ES-ABC (c/n 26324) is seen at Amsterdam-Schiphol in August 1997.

Below: The majority of Liverpool-based **Emerald Airways** operation is freight. However a passenger service between base and the Isle of Man is operated using BAe ATPs. G-JEMA (c/n 2028) is pictured landing at Liverpool in June 2004.

Above: **El Dorado Colombia** was one of the many general cargo operators to be found at Villavicencio. Douglas DC-3 HK-122 (c/n 4414) is seen at base in September 1997. The carrier suspended services during 1999.

Left: Dubai-based **Emirates Airlines** is a large Middle Eastern carrier renowned for its excellent cabin service. Airbus A310-308 A6-EKP (c/n 695) lands at Zürich in August 1998.

Swiss holiday charter company **Edelweiss Air** is owned by Kuoni, a world-leading tour operator. With a fleet of Airbus aircraft it covers the sunspots of Europe and beyond from its Zürich base. Airbus A320-214 HB-IHX (c/n 942) is seen climbing out of Palma, Majorca in September 2000.

Spanish carrier **ERA – European Regions Airlines** flew a pair of Brazilian regional jets. Embraer RJ145EU EC-GZU (c/n 145106) lands at the company base, Palma, Majorca in September 2000. The following month the company suspended operations and filed for bankruptcy.

Left: Executive Aerospace is a Durban-based South African carrier with a fleet of six 748s. Hawker Siddeley (Avro) 748 Srs.2B ZS-NNW (c/n 1785) is pictured at base in November 1998. (RO'B)

Above left: The Evergreen group of companies have many aviation-related operations. One of these is aerial fire fighting with water bombers. Sikorsky S-64E Skycrane N6979R (c/n 64079) is operated by **Evergreen Helicopters**. It is seen at Chico, California in October 2001. The large tank under the fuselage is for the fire-fighting role.

Above right: Express One International was a Dallas-based cargo line with a fleet of 727s. McDonnell Douglas DC-10-30 F-OKBB (c/n 46981) was chartered to the company in 1993/4 and put in full livery. It is pictured on take-off at Miami, April 1994. Operations were suspended in 2002.

Right: El Al is the flag carrier for the state of Israel. Boeing 767-27E 4X-EAE (c/n 24832) shows the airline's new livery at Bangkok in November 1999.

British carrier **Euroceltic Airways** was based in Waterford, Ireland. They had a fleet of two F.27s. Fokker F.27-500RF Friendship G-ECAH (c/n 10669) is seen on a passenger charter to Fairford in July 2002. In January of the following year operations were suspended.

As can be seen from their livery, **Eastern Australia Airlines** is part of the Qantas group. It flies commuter services around New South Wales. De Havilland Canada DHC-8 Dash 8-102 VH-TQU (c/n 346) is seen at Sydney in September 2000. (RO'B)

Left: European Air Charter is a UK operator that specialises in leasing aircraft to airlines and holiday companies. Boeing 747-236B G-BDXJ (c/n 21831) is seen at Manchester in August 2002.

Below: Evergreen International Airlines is a Marana, Arizona-based cargo carrier with DC-9 and 747 aircraft. DC-9-32F N935F (c/n 47220) is seen on the move at Phoenix in October 1998.

Above: The sole 707 left in **Egyptair's** service is configured as a freighter. Boeing 707-366C SU-APD (c/n 20341) climbs out of Sharjah, UAE in March 2000.

Below: Showing off the new livery of Egypt's flag carrier **Egyptair** is wide-body Airbus A340-212 SU-GBM (c/n 156). It is seen on approach to London-Heathrow in July 1997.

Milan-based **Eurofly,** is part of the Alitalia group. This is reflected in their livery. Airbus A320-214 I-BIKD (c/n 1457) is seen landing at Manchester in May 2003 on a football charter.

Left: Frontier Flying Services is an Alaskan passenger and freight carrier based at Fairbanks. They have a mixed fleet of aircraft with a seating capacity up to nineteen. Beech 1900C Airliner N575P (c/n UC-95) is at base in May 2000.

Below: Denver-based **Frontier Airlines** – The Spirit of the West – has different animal pictures on each side of the fin. Boeing 737-201 N217US (c/n 20215) shows its eagle motif at Phoenix in October 1998.

Spanish holiday charter line **Futura International Airways** is a subsidiary of Aer Lingus. EC-GNZ Boeing 737-4Y0 (c/n 25178) is seen departing the carrier's Palma base in September 2000, in the company's latest livery.

Above: Malmo-based **Falcon Air** has a fleet of three 737s. By day they fly holiday charters and by night mail, as the airline is owned by the Swedish Post Office. Boeing 737-33A SE-DPA (c/n 25401) is at Palma, Majorca in September 2000.

Brazilian passenger carrier **Fly SA** (Linhas Aereas) were based in São Paulo and operated three 727s when services were suspended in 2003. Boeing 727-227 PP-JUB (c/n 21242) is seen stored at base in April 2004. (RO'B)

Right: Flyjet is a UK holiday charter operator with a fleet of two 757s. Boeing 757-23A G-FJEA (c/n 24636) lines up to depart from Manchester in August 2003.

Left: FedEx have cornered the market with the MD-11; they currently operate 42. This is in addition to their DC-10 fleet. McDonnell Douglas MD-11F N587FE (c/n 48489) departs from Sharjah, UAE in March 2000.

Below: The first Airbus, the A300, has found a new lease of life with conversions to carry freight and as new-build cargo aircraft. Airbus A300-605F N668FE (c/n 772) of FedEx is in the latter group. It is pictured on the ramp at Minneapolis-St Paul in May 2000.

Fischer Air is a Prague-based holiday charter company flying Czech citizens to European sunspots. Boeing 737-33A OK-FAN (c/n 27469) lifts off from Palma, Majorca in September 2000, in a very distinctive livery.

Freedom Air is a low-cost subsidiary of Air New Zealand. It operates domestic and regional international services with a fleet of 737s. Boeing 737-3K2 ZK-SJE (c/n 27635) is seen at Brisbane following a service across the Tasman Sea to Australia in February 2003.

Above: First Air is a Canadian carrier who flies both passengers and freight services using a mixed fleet of ten types from a Beaver to a 727. Hawker Siddeley (Avro) 748-215 Srs.2A C-GDUN (c/n 1581) is seen outside its hangar at Yellowknife in May 2000.

Right: Pictured at Red Deer, Alberta in May 2000 is Lockheed L-188A Electra 9Q-CDU (c/n 1040) in the full livery of Filair. This carrier is based in Kinshasa, Democratic Republic of Congo. The operator had passed the aircraft on to Air Spray for water-bomber conversion.

One of Bolivia's premier meat-freight operators was **Fri Reyes** (Frigorifico Reyes). Douglas DC-4 CP-1207 (c/n 10790) is on the ramp at the carrier's base, La Paz in November 1992. Services were suspended in 1994.

Above: **Fairlines** was a French regional airline with a pair of Luxembourg-registered aircraft. McDonnell Douglas MD-81 LX-FAB (c/n 48058) is at London-Gatwick in September 1998. The Paris CDG-based carrier suspended operations in November of that year. (SGW)

Left: **First Choice Airways** is the new name for UK holiday charter operator Air 2000. The name reflects the holiday marketing name used. Boeing 757-2Y0(ER) G-OOOX (c/n 26158) is seen about to depart Manchester in April 2004.

Below: **Flying Finn Airways** was a short-lived low-cost operator with a fleet of two aircraft based at Helsinki. McDonnell Douglas MD-83 OH-LMR (c/n 49284) is seen about to land at London-Stansted in August 2003. January of the following year saw the end of services.

First Cambodian Airlines was based in the capital, Phnom Penh and operated a single aircraft. Airbus A320-232 S7-RGL (c/n 542) is seen at Singapore-Changi in May 2004. In August of that year services were suspended and the aircraft returned to the leasing company. (RO'B)

Peruvian carrier **Faucett** had been founded in 1928 and so it was a sad day in September 1997 when an airline with such a long history ceased flying. Pictured at Miami in November 1992, is Lockheed L-1011 TriStar 1 OB-1504 (c/n 1087).

Florida Air Transport is an ad hoc freight charter carrier. Douglas DC-6A N766WC (c/n 44597) is seen at the company base, Fort Lauderdale Executive in October 1998.

Above: **Forest Industries Flying Tankers** flies the last two Mars flying boats in a water-bomber role. These magnificent machines skim a lake to collect up to 6,000 gallons in 22 seconds. The drop area is 250 feet wide and 800 feet long. Martin JRM-3 Mars C-FLYK (c/n 76820) is seen at its Sproat Lake, Vancouver Island, base in May 2000.

Left: The national airline of Finland is **Finnair**. It has a history dating back to 1923. Pictured at Bangkok in November 1999 is the largest type in the fleet, McDonnell Douglas MD-11. OH-LGD (c/n 48513) is seen arriving at its gate.

Below: Commuter services for **Finnair** are flown mainly by the ATR 72-201. OH-KRA (c/n 126) is seen on a domestic service at Tikkakoski in June 1998.

Above: Showing the new livery of **Finnair** is Boeing 757-2Q8 OH-LBR (c/n 28167). It is seen departing Palma, Majorca in September 2000.

Right: **Finnaviation** was a subsidiary of Finnair, flying commuter and feeder services. SAAB 340B OH-FAF (c/n 340B-167) is seen at the company base, Helsinki in June 1998. This aircraft was awaiting a repaint as the airline had been merged into the parent company in September 1996.

Above left: UK holiday charter company **Flying Colours** was based at Manchester. Boeing 757-25F G-FCLD (c/n 28718) is on pushback at Newcastle in May 1997. The company was part of the Thomas Cook empire and was merged into the new house airline JMC Airlines in March 2000.

Above right: The **FRAM** on this new-generation Boeing 737-85F F-GRNA (c/n 28823) relates to the French tour operator Voyages FRAM. The aircraft, pictured at Palma, Majorca in September 2000, is operated by Euralair International to fly holiday charters.

Left: **Fly FTI** was a German holiday charter line owned by Frosch Touristik International. UK operator Airtours owned 29% of the carrier hence the house style livery. Airbus A320-231 D-ACAF (c/n 444), one of a fleet of six, is seen at Frankfurt in June 1999. In November 2001 services were suspended.

Right: Pictured at Tenerife in the Canary Islands in June 2004 is Boeing 737-31S G-OTDA (c/n 29266) of **FlyGlobeSpan**. This is a Scottish-based low-cost and holiday charter airline. (JDS)

Below left: Turkish operator **Free Bird Airlines** is based in Istanbul. McDonnell Douglas MD-83 TC-FBT (c/n 49949) is seen at Manchester in August 2004.

Below right: **Fair** operates a fleet of four Regional Jets for ANA as a feeder operator. Seen at Osaka-Itami in October 2004 is Canadair CJR 200ER JA03RJ (c/n 7624).

Above: Once part of the Soviet Union, the Republic of Georgia is now independent. **Georgian Airlines – Airzena** is the main carrier for flights to Western Europe. Boeing 737-5K5 D-AHLI (c/n 25037) is pictured at Frankfurt in June 2001.

Garuda Indonesia is owned by the government and is the flag carrier for the nation. It operates a modern fleet mix of Boeing and Airbus types. Services are flown worldwide. Boeing 737-4U3 PK-GWQ (c/n 25719) is seen at Singapore-Changi in February 2003.

Below: Once based at Newcastle in the north-east of England, **Gill Airways** had a wide domestic route network. ATR 42-300 G-BXBV (c/n 245) is pictured at base in May 1997. In September 2001 operations were suspended.

Gulfstream International Airlines is a Florida-based commuter carrier. De Havilland Canada DHC-7 Dash 7-102 N4860J (c/n 19) is seen landing at Miami in October 1998.

Right: Turkish charter company **GTI Airlines** was an all-Airbus operator based at Antalya. Airbus A300B4-103 TC-GTA (c/n 054) is pictured at Düsseldorf in June 1997. February of the following year saw a change of name to Anatolia. (JDS)

Below: **Green Airways** of Red Lake Sea Plane Base, Ontario, is one of many Canadian floatplane operators specialising in services for fishermen wanting to travel to lodges on remote lakes. De Havilland Canada DHC-3 Otter C-FLEA (c/n 286) is seen at base in June 1990.

Gull Airways was a US east coast-based commuter airline. N130EM Embraer EMB-110P1 Bandeirante (c/n 110416) is at Boston in August 1986. Operations were suspended in March 1997.

Minneapolis-based **Gemini Air Cargo** is an all-freight operator with a DC-10 and MD-11 fleet mix. McDonnell Douglas DC-10-30F N605GC (c/n 47925) is seen departing Lima, Peru in September 1997.

Greenlandair is base at Nuuk. Most of the fleet are helicopters and STOL commuters. The one jet in the fleet is Boeing 757-236 OY-GRL (c/n 25620). It is seen at Frankfurt in June 1999.

Above left: Set up by British Airways as a low-cost subsidiary, **Go Fly** operated a wide range of scheduled European services from its base at Stansted. Boeing 737-3Y0 G-IGOA (c/n 24678) is at Palma, Majorca in September 2000. Each aircraft had a different name for instance, 'Let's Go' and a different colour scheme. The airline was bought by and merged into easyJet in March 2003.

Above right: The French-built Caravelle is becoming a rare sight today. Operated by **Gabon Express** of Libreville is Sud Aviation SE-210 Caravelle 11R 3D-CAN (c/n 240). It is used as a combi for both freight and passengers and is pictured at Rand, South Africa in December 1999. (RO'B)

Left: German charter carrier **Germania** has added a low-cost no-frills side to its business. A fleet of ex-American Airlines Fokker 100s flies this part of the operation. D-AGPN (c/n 11333) is pictured at Berlin-Tegel in May 2004.

GMC Airlines is one of two commuter lines in Bangladesh. De Havilland Canada DHC-8 Dash 8-102 S2-ACZ (c/n 251) is seen at its Dhaka base in December 1999. (RO'B)

Gulf Air is the national airline for Bahrain, Oman, and Abu Dhabi. They have an extensive network both east and west of their Bahrain base. The fleet is a mix of Boeing and Airbus types. Airbus A340-312 A40-LD (c/n 097) is seen at Hong Kong in March 2003.

Right: Hemet Valley Flying Services was for many years one of the leading American water-bomber operators. Fairchild C-119C N13742 (c/n 10431) is seen on duty at Santa Barbara in October 1979 at the California Department of Forestry Air Attack Base. The company suspended operations in 1997.

Hawkins & Powers of Greybull, Wyoming is the operator of the only C-97 water-bomber. Boeing C-97G N1365N (c/n 16729) is seen on its arrival day at Fort Wainwright, Alaska in May 2000, to start its summer forest guard duty.

The large Russian transport helicopters are popular in Peru with both civil and military operators. **Helisur (Helicopteros del Sur)** of Iquitos operates a fleet of four. Mil Mi-17 OB-1584 (c/n 95432) is seen at Lima in September 2003.

Henson Airlines was based at Salisbury, Maryland. It was a commuter operator flying services for Piedmont. De Havilland Canada DHC-8 Dash 8-102 N916HA (c/n 072) is seen at Washington-National in May 1989. The company is now part of US Air Express.

Above: Pictured at its Vancouver Harbour base in April 2003, is de Havilland Canada DHC-3 Turbo Otter C-GVNL (c/n 105) of **Harbour Air**. This carrier operates regular scheduled services to locations on Vancouver Island. Note this is one of the relatively rare turbo conversions of the Otter. (RO'B)

Right: Helios Airways of Larnaca, Cyprus, is a charter operator which flies holidaymakers from northern Europe to its Mediterranean island base. Boeing 737-86N 5B-DBI (c/n 30807) displays the company's attractive livery at Manchester in April 2002.

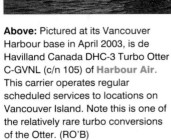

Following the Shorts Belfast's retirement from the Royal Air Force, **Heavylift Cargo Airlines** of Stansted became its sole operator, flying worldwide charters using the its vast bulk capacity. Shorts SC.5 Belfast G-BFYU (c/n SH1821) climbs out of Fairford in July 1987. The carrier ceased operations in September 2002 and, following a period of storage, one of the company Belfasts was sold to an Australian operator with the same name.

Above: Haines Airways is based in the town of Haines, Alaska. It is a small air taxi and general charter operator with a fleet of Cherokee and Navajo aircraft. Piper PA-31 Navajo N27726 (c/n 31-7852125) is pictured at Anchorage in May 2000.

Left: Heavylift Cargo Airlines operated three Airbus freighters. They also were known for their wet leasing of the giant Antonov An-124 when required. Airbus A300B4-203(F) G-HLAB (c/n 045) is seen at Frankfurt in June 2001. Operations closed in September of the following year.

Helicol (Helicopteros Nacionales de Colombia) is involved with both fixed- and rotary-wing operations in support of the oil industry. Bell 206L Long Ranger HK-3727-X is seen at Bogota in November 1992.

Above: The German tour operator TUI set up **Hapag-Lloyd Express** at the end of 2002. The bright livery is to represent a New York taxi. Boeing 737-5K5 D-AHLN (c/n 25062) is seen departing Manchester in April 2004.

Right: Based in Hanover, German carrier **Hapag-Lloyd** is a major holiday charter operator. They have a fleet of 737 and A310 airliners. Airbus A310-204 D-AHLW (c/n 427) is pictured on approach to Palma, Majorca in September 2000.

Above left: Horizon Air is a major Seattle-based commuter operator with a large fleet of Dash 8 and F.28 aircraft. De Havilland Canada DHC-8 Dash 8-102 N814PH (c/n 043) is pictured at Vancouver in August 1992. (RO'B)

Above right: Hamburg International is a German holiday charter operator with six new-generation 737s. Pictured at Manchester in March 2003 is Boeing 737-73S D-AHID (c/n 29080).

Right: Another Horizon, this one is Australian cargo and passenger carrier **Horizon Airlines**. Hawker Siddeley (Avro) 748-287 Srs.2B VH-IMK (c/n 1737) is seen at its Sydney-Bankstown base in May 2000. (RO'B)

Above left: Hunting Cargo Airlines was the last operator of the Vanguard. Vickers 953C Vanguard (Merchantman) G-APES (c/n 721) is seen at Dublin in June 1994. The carrier, based at East Midlands, transferred its operation to Ireland and was renamed Air Contractors.

Above right: Hispania is one of many Spanish holiday charter operators that have come and gone. Boeing 757-23A EC-EMV (c/n 23289) is seen at East Midlands in June 1989. The following month the airline suspended services.

Right: Helvetic Airways is a Swiss scheduled passenger carrier. It used to be known as Odette Airways and adopted the new name in 2004. Fokker 100 HB-JVD (c/n 11498) is at the carrier's Zürich base in September 2004 in the very distinctive livery of the company.

Right: East Germany, the old GDR, had **Interflug** as its sole airline. Ilyushin IL-18D D-AOAU (c/n 188010904) is seen at Fairford operating flights for Berline in July 1991. By then, the reunification of Germany had spelt an end to the carrier and its fleet of Russian-built aircraft.

Below left: The last commercial operator of the Bristol Freighter in the UK was **Instone Airlines**. They specialised in the carriage of racehorses. Bristol B.170 Freighter Mk.31 G-BISU (c/n 13218) is seen at Stansted in July 1982. The company ceased aircraft services in 1984.

Above right: Looking the worst for wear is **Imperial Air** Antonov An-32 OB-1603 (c/n 2603) at Lima in September 1997. The Peruvian airline operated a mix of Soviet designs, the An-32 and the Tu-134. Services had been suspended in January of that year and the fleet was in store.

Left: Pictured at Melbourne in April 1988, is Armstrong-Whitworth Argosy 101 VH-IPD (c/n 6656) of **IPEC** (Interstate Parcel Express Company). It had formed an aviation division to operate a regular service from Melbourne to Tasmania. Operations were suspended in 1993. (RO'B)

Below left: **IFG Inter Regional** was a German domestic passenger carrier. Nord 262A-30 D-CADY (c/n 37) is seen on the ramp at Düsseldorf in July 1970.

Above right: The Cessna 310G has a capacity for five passengers. EI-ATC (c/n 310G-0050) of **Iona National Airways** is on the apron at Liverpool-Speke in April 1986. The Dublin-based air taxi and charter company ceased operations at the end of 1994.

Left: **ICC – Air Cargo Canada** is an all-Airbus equipped freight carrier based at Toronto. Airbus A300B4-203 C-GICR (c/n 183) is pictured arriving at Vancouver in May 2000.

Left: British holiday charter company **Inter European Airways** was based at Cardiff in Wales. Boeing 737-3Y0 G-BNGM (c/n 23925) lands at Manchester in March 1991. The carrier was taken over by Airtours in November 1993.

Below: Showing off a smart new livery for **Intercontinental Colombia** is de Havilland Canada DHC-8 Dash 8-300 HK-4062X (c/n 196). It is pictured on the ramp at Bogota in September 1997.

Indonesian Airlines is a small passenger carrier based in the capital, Jakarta. The fleet is just two first-generation Boeing jets. Pictured at Berlin-Schönefeld in May 2004 is Boeing 737-330 D-ABXF (c/n 23527) following the termination of a lease.

International Air Response is the new name for Arizona water-bomber company T&G Aviation. Pictured in May 2000, at Palmer, Alaska, is Douglas DC-7B N4887C (c/n 45351). The immaculate propliner is in a colour scheme as used by Delta in the 1950s. It is on station for the summer to protect against forest fires. Note the belly tank for the chemical fire retardant.

Above: Pictured on take-off at Palma, Majorca in September 2000 is Boeing 757-27B TF-FIW (c/n 24838) of **Icelandair**, displaying the new livery for the airline. It is also marked 'Holidays' as the carrier has a subsidiary company selling tours to the North Atlantic island.

Right: **Ilavia** is an associate company of the Russian Ilyushin Design Bureau which operates cargo flights. Ilyushin IL-18V RA-75811 (c/n 182004504) is at Sharjah, UAE in March 1997. The home base is Moscow-Zhukovsky.

IAC – Integrated Aviation Consortium is set up to provide a group of oil companies with flights. Flightline provides the aircraft. Pictured in IAC livery is BAe 146-200 G-TBIC (c/n E2025) at Manchester in August 2003.

The Spanish flag carrier is Iberia (Lineas Aereas de Espana SA). They fly worldwide. Boeing 747-256B EC-DIB (c/n 22239) is pictured departing the carrier's Madrid base in September 2002.

Right: Australian regional passenger carrier Impulse Airlines had progressed from a prop-only fleet of Beech 1900s with the arrival of jets. Boeing 717-23S VH-SMH (c/n 55063) is at the company base, Sydney in September 2000. Australian flag carrier Qantas bought the airline and renamed it Jetstar, as its new low-cost arm. (RO'B)

The majority of the services flown by Indian Airlines are domestic. Some regional international routes are served. Airbus A320-231 VT-EPL (c/n 074) is seen at Bangkok in January 2002. It is of note that the first batch of A320s Indian bought had a double-bogie undercarriage. This was in order to handle poor runway surfaces.

Above: Many airliners today are owned by leasing companies. Most, however, do not have any external indication of ownership. An exception to this is Lockheed L-1011 TriStar 200 N104NL (c/n 1203) of Interlease Aviation Group; note the logo on the middle engine. It is seen at East Midlands in July 2000.

The airline Iberworld is owned by Spanish tour operator Grupo Viajes Iberia. The carrier flies charters around northern Europe. Airbus A320-214 EC-GZD (c/n 879) climbs out of its Palma, Majorca base in September 2000.

State-owned Iran Air flies domestic, Middle and Far Eastern and European passenger services. Airbus A300-605R EP-IBB (c/n 727) is at Frankfurt, June 1999.

JAT (Jugoslovenski Aero Transport) was the national carrier for what is now a much smaller country than when it was formed in 1947. Boeing 727-2H9 YU-AKG (c/n 21039) is seen landing at Manchester in April 1991.

Above: **Jersey European Airways** is not based on the Channel Island of Jersey, but at Exeter in the south-west of England. It is a growing regional carrier with both domestic and international services. Fokker F.27 Friendship 500RF G-JEAI (c/n 10672) is at Birmingham in November 1996. The airline changed its name, in June 2000, to British European Airways to reflect its wider route network.

Left: **JAS – Japan Air System** is a mainly domestic carrier with a small number of international services. Airbus A300-622R JA8562 (c/n 679) is on the move at Xian, China in October 1999. It wears the old style livery of the company. The carrier has been taken over by Japan Air Lines and its fleet is being repainted in JAL colours.

Below: The Japanese flag carrier is **JAL – Japan Airlines**. Services are flown worldwide. McDonnell Douglas MD-11 JA8583 (c/n 48574) is pictured, in the old livery, on approach to Frankfurt in June 1997.

Above: **Jet Airways** is a growing Indian regional carrier based at Mumbai. Pictured at Sharjah, UAE, on delivery in March 2000, is ATR 72-212A F-WQMC/VT-JCD (c/n 636).

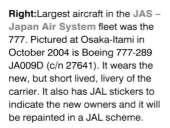

Right: Largest aircraft in the **JAS – Japan Air System** fleet was the 777. Pictured at Osaka-Itami in October 2004 is Boeing 777-289 JA009D (c/n 27641). It wears the new, but short lived, livery of the carrier. It also has JAL stickers to indicate the new owners and it will be repainted in a JAL scheme.

Pictured at Tokyo-Narita in October 2004 is **JAL Cargo** Boeing 747-221F JA8160 (c/n 21744). This aircraft, one of a number of freight Jumbos in the carrier's fleet, wears the new livery of the airline.

Above: J.A.M. Air is the aviation department of the Jesus Alive Ministries. Hawker Siddeley (Avro) 780 Andover 3C-JJX (c/n Set 6) is at base in December 1999. The charity is based at Lanseria in South Africa despite the registration of Equatorial Guinea. The short-field performance of the Andover is ideal for relief work at remote African sites. (RO'B)

Left: One of the most original civil air transport operations is that of **JU-Air** of Switzerland. The carrier flies original, 1939 built, Junkers Ju-52/3Ms on sightseeing tours through the Alps. HB-HOS (c/n 6580) is seen at the airline's Dubendorf base in September 2004.

Right: JMC Air, owned by the Thomas Cook Group, was formed in 2000 by amalgamating Caledonian and Flying Colours. The JMC is John Mason Cook, the founder's son. G-BXKD Airbus A320-214 (c/n 735) climbs off runway 06R at Palma Majorca in September 2000. This operating company was short lived as in April 2003 it was rebranded as Thomas Cook Airlines.

Below: Jetcraft Aviation is an Australian mixed freight and passenger carrier operating a fleet of ten Metros. Swearingen SA-226TC Metro II VH-UZQ (c/n TC-259) is pictured at the company base, Brisbane-Archerfield in February 2003.

An all-cargo airline, **Johnsons Air** of Accra, Ghana, flies ad hoc charters. Boeing 707-324C 9G-OLD (c/n 19350) is at Sharjah, UAE in March 2000.

Above left: Originally known as Impulse Airlines, Jetstar Airways has been set up by Qantas as a low-cost carrier. Airbus A320-232 VH-JQG (c/n 2169) is at Sydney-Kingsford Smith in October 2004.

Above right: JTA – Japan TransOcean Air is a member of the JAL group of airlines. Based on the southern island of Okinawa, it has an all-737 fleet. Boeing 737-429 JA8931 (c/n 25247) is seen arriving at its gate, at base, in October 2004.

Left: Based in Osaka, JAL Express is a subsidiary of JAL and operates an all-737 fleet. Boeing 737-446 JA8994 (c/n 28097) is seen at Okinawa in October 2004.

Above left: Hiroshima-based J-Air is a JAL-owned commuter operator. Canadair CRJ200ER JA204J (c/n 7643) is seen at Osaka-Itami in October 2004.

Above right: JALways used to be known as Japan Air Charter; it is part of the JAL group. Boeing 747-346 JA8186 (c/n 24018) is pictured landing at Osaka-Kansai in October 2004. The aircraft wears the colourful *Reso'cha* scheme of flowers and birds.

Right: A subsidiary of JAL, Japan Air Commuter is based at Kagoshima. It flies a mixed fleet of Swedish, Japanese and Canadian built aircraft. SAAB 340B JA8642 (c/n 340B-365) is pictured at Nagasaki in October 2004.

This Lockheed L-188A Electra N5511 (c/n 1016) is operated at the **Kwajalein Missile Range,** in the Pacific Ocean, by the US Navy. It is seen at Oakland, California in October 1979.

Keen Airways is based at Liverpool. Its two passenger aircraft are usually found at Blackpool operating a service to the Isle of Man. Embraer EMB-110P1 Bandeirante G-BGYT (c/n 110234) is seen at Blackpool in March 2004.

A rare type to be seen on floats is the Aztec. Piper PA-23 Aztec-D N14BP (c/n 27-4279) is seen at Lake Hood, Anchorage in May 2000. It is operated by **Kenai Fjords Air Service** of Homer-Beluga Sea Plane Base. This company operates during the summer months only.

Above: Kras Air (Krasnoyarsk Airlines) is a mixed Russian passenger and cargo carrier. The fleet mix has begun to include western-built aircraft. Tupolev Tu-154M RA-85694 (c/n 867) is seen at Frankfurt in June 2001.

Below: Kirov Air Enterprise is a mixed passenger, freight and utility company based in the city of Kirov. Tupolev Tu-134A RA-65060 (c/n 49872) is at Moscow-Domodedovo in August 1997. (JDS)

Above: Kelner Airways was a Canadian general cargo carrier based at Pickle Lake in northern Ontario. Cessna 208 Caravan 1 C-FKAL (c/n 208-00124) is seen at base in June 1990. The airline was renamed Wasaya Airways at the start of 1993.

Right: Kulula.Com is the low-cost no-frills airline set up by Comair of South Africa. Boeing 727-230 ZS-NOV (c/n 21114) is pictured at Cape Town in April 2001. Kulula is the Zulu word for 'easy'. (RO'B)

Above left: From Kogalym in the Tyumen region of Russia comes **Kolavia**. The fleet mix is of Mi-8 helicopters and passenger-equipped Tu-134 & 154 airliners. Seen at Sharjah, UAE in March 2000, is Tupolev Tu-154M RA-85787 (c/n 971).

Above right: With a stunning livery **KMV** (Kavkazskie Mineralnye Vody) of Russia operate a fleet of Tu-134, 154 and 204 airliners. Tupolev Tu-154B-2 RA-85457 (c/n 457) is photographed on the ramp at Sharjah, UAE in March 2000.

Left: Russian operator **Kuban Airlines** is based at Krasnodar. The fleet comprises mainly passenger-configured An-24s and Yak-42s. Yakovlev Yak-42D RA-42367 (c/n 4520421914133) is seen arriving at Frankfurt in June 1999.

Right: **KTHY – Cyprus Turkish Airlines** is the carrier for the Turkish Republic of North Cyprus, a state is recognised only by Turkey. Associated with Turkish Airlines, KTHY have a mixed Boeing and Airbus fleet. Boeing 737-8S3 TC-MZZ (c/n 29247) is pictured at Manchester in June 2002.

Below left: The former Soviet Republic of Kyrgyzstan has one main air transport company at the capital, Bishkek. This operates aircraft ranging from utility An-2 aircraft up to IL-76 freighters. Tupolev Tu-154M EX-85762 (c/n 945) lands at Frankfurt in June 1997, in the markings of **Kyrghyzstan Airlines**.

Below right: Another former Soviet republic is Kazakstan. Tupolev Tu-154B-2 UN-85396 (c/n 396) is at Sharjah, UAE, in March 1997 with **Kazakstan Airlines** titles. This carrier ceased operations and now flies as Air Kazakstan.

Above left: Kampuchea Airlines was a Cambodian passenger carrier with a fleet of TriStars. Lockheed L-1011 TriStar 50 XU-300 (c/n 1129) is seen arriving at Bangkok in February 2001. The following year all services were suspended.

Above right: Kuwait Airways is the sole airline in the state. They have a wide network of scheduled routes with a very modern fleet of Boeing and Airbus airliners. Boeing 777-269 9K-AOB (c/n 28744) is on pushback at Frankfurt in June 1999.

Left: Kendell Airlines was based in the Australian town of Wagga Wagga. It operated domestic commuter services with a fleet of Metros, SAABs and CRJs. Swearingen SA.227DC Metro 23 VH-KEU (c/n DC-846B) is seen at Melbourne-Tullamarine in October 1999. (RO'B) The carrier was merged into REX-Regional Express in August 2002.

Above left: Pictured on the ramp at Detroit-Willow Run in June 1990 is Kalitta Douglas DC-8-55F N855BC (c/n 45804). The carrier specialised in motor industry charters, and was renamed American International and then Kitty Hawk.

Above right: KLM uk was the result of the takeover of Air UK. The company operated domestic and international routes as well as feeder flights for the parent company. Fokker 50 G-UKTD (c/n 20256) is seen at Düsseldorf in September 1998. The carrier was merged into the Dutch airline KLM Cityhopper in 2003.

Right: Dutch carrier KLM operates both 200 and 400 series Jumbos in the freight role. KLM Cargo Boeing 747-206B(SF) PH-BUH (c/n 21110) is seen arriving at Singapore-Changi in February 2003.

Left: KLM (Koninklijke Luchtvaart Maatschappij) has a history dating back to 1919. The Dutch national carrier is known worldwide. Boeing 737-406 PH-BDR (c/n 24514) is seen at the company base, Amsterdam-Schiphol in August 1997. In 2004 the airline merged with Air France but will keep its own identity.

Below: Since the government of Algeria has allowed more airlines to be formed in the country there have been several newcomers. One such was **Khalifa Airways**, based in the city of Algiers. Services operated to a number of French cities and other European locations. Airbus A310-324ET F-OGYN (c/n 458) is pictured on a late Sunday evening service to Palma, Majorca in September 2000. The carrier suspended all services in April 2003. (JDS)

KLM Asia is a subsidiary formed to operate services to Taiwan without upsetting the government in Beijing. Boeing 747-406 PH-BFC (c/n 23982) is under tow at Amsterdam-Schiphol in August 1997.

The largest airline in Korea is **Korean Air**, with a fleet of more than a hundred aircraft in service or on order. It flies worldwide. Boeing 777-38B HL7573 (c/n 27953) is seen at Hong Kong in March 2003.

Above: Russian passenger carrier **Karat** has the usual mix of locally-built aircraft in its fleet. Yakovlev Yak-42D RA-42402 (c/n 4520422116583) is seen at its Moscow-Vnukovo base in August 1997. (JDS)

Right: Korean Air Cargo operates four MD-11s in a freight-only role, the type is not used for any passenger services. McDonnell Douglas MD-11F HL7372 (c/n 48408) is seen at Shanghai in October 1999.

Lotus Air is an Egyptian passenger company with a fleet of five single-aisle Airbus aircraft. Seen on the runway at Frankfurt in June 1999, is Airbus A320-212 SU-LBB (c/n 814).

Like a number of airlines in South America **LAB – Lloyd Aereo Boliviano** has a long history; it dates back to 1925. Pictured at La Paz in November 1992, is Boeing 727-2K3 CP-1276 (c/n 21082).

Laker Airways was a British holiday charter line founded by Mr (now Sir) Freddie Laker in 1966. Pictured at Palma, Majorca in November 1973, is Douglas DC-10-10 G-AZZD (c/n 46906). It has extra 'Skytrain' titles, his low-cost transatlantic service. The carrier suspended services in 1982 but formed a new Bahamas-based company in 1992.

LACSA Costa Rica is a member of the TACA group of airlines hence the common basic livery. Boeing 737-2L9 N281LF (c/n 22071) lands at Miami in October 1998, on a scheduled service from the Central American republic.

Larry's Flying Service is a small Fairbanks, Alaska-based general charter company, with types ranging from a Cherokee to a King Air. Britten-Norman BN-2B-21 Islander N414JA (c/n 2107) is seen at base in May 2000.

Another Lotus but this is **Lotus Airways** a Sharjah UAE-based cargo line with a single aircraft registered in Equatorial Guinea. Antonov An-12B 3C-ZZD (c/n 00347305) is pictured on the ramp at base in March 2000.

South African carrier **Luft Afrique** flies a mix of passengers and cargo with its four F.27s. Pictured at Pretoria-Wonderboom in August 2000, is Fokker F.27 Troopship 300M ZS-OEK (c/n 10161). The Troopship is the military variant of the Friendship, having a large cargo door and strengthened floor. (RO'B)

Lions Air of Switzerland's prime role is operating Pilatus PC-12s under a fractional ownership agreement. They also operate a single Dornier Do 328 HB-AEE (c/n 3005). This 32-seat airliner is pictured at the company base, Zürich in September 2004.

Argentine carrier LAER – Lineas Aereas Entre Rios operates a single Fokker F.28-1000 Fellowship jointly with American Falcon. LV-LZN (c/n 11048) is pictured on the ramp at Buenos Aires-Aeroparque J Newbery in October 2003.

Lynden Air Cargo is an all-freight carrier based at Anchorage, Alaska. Lockheed L-100-30 Hercules N404LC (c/n 4763) is seen on the move at Elmendorf Air Force Base, near Anchorage in May 2000.

Vienna-based charter and scheduled carrier Lauda Air was formed by Formula 1 racing driver Niki Lauda. It has grown to operate worldwide holiday flights and is now totally owned by Austrian Airlines. Boeing 777-2Z9 OE-LPB (c/n 28699) lands at Miami in October 1998.

Left: The Boeing 737 is not the most common freight aircraft despite being the most successful jet airliner built. Boeing 737-204 CC-CSD (c/n 20417) of LAN Chile Cargo is seen at the carrier's Santiago base in October 2003.

Below: Showing off its smart new livery is LAN Chile Boeing 767-316(ER) CC-CZT (c/n 29228) as it departs its Santiago base in October 2003. The Chilean national airline dates back to 1929 and now just uses the name LAN.

It is quite common for an established airline to set up a low-cost operation. Such a company is LAN Chile Express. It flies a mixed fleet of single-aisle Boeing and Airbus types from the capital city, Santiago. Boeing 737-2Q3 CC-CVI (c/n 22367) is seen at base in October 2003 and shows the different livery.

Right: German flag carrier **Lufthansa** is known worldwide. It operates a variety of Airbus types. Airbus A340-211 D-AIBE (c/n 019) is seen at Frankfurt in June 1997.

Below: The Fokker Friendship was licence built in the USA by Fairchild. Seen in store at Tamiami, Florida in October 1998 is Fairchild F-27A YN-CER (c/n 30) of Nicaraguan carrier **LADECA**.

Lion Airlines is a growing Indonesian low-cost carrier operating domestic and regional international services. Boeing 737-4Y0 PK-LIF (c/n 24467) is seen arriving at Singapore-Changi in August 2004. (RO'B)

Lufthansa Cargo operates a type not in service with the main company, the MD-11. Pictured at one of its main hubs, Sharjah, UAE in March 2000, is McDonnell Douglas MD-11F D-ALCE (c/n 48785).

Above: Pictured at the carrier's Antigua base in June 1983, is de Havilland Canada DHC-6 Twin Otter 300 V2-LCK (c/n 762) of **LIAT – The Caribbean Airline**. The company flies services around the region. The LIAT name was derived from Leeward Islands Air Transport. (RO'B)

Right: With an ever-changing airline market some of South America's take-offare setting up subsidiary operators in neighbouring countries. Chile has set up **LAN Peru**. Airbus A320-233 VP-BCJ (c/n 1491) is seen about to depart its Lima base in October 2003. Note that the livery is similar to the parent carrier with just a name change.

LTU International Airways of Düsseldorf is one of the major German holiday charter operators. Boeing 757-225 D-AMUK (c/n 22689) is seen at Frankfurt's Terminal 2 in June 1999.

Colombian passenger carrier Latina de Aviacion has a fleet of two aircraft. The larger is a Douglas DC-3. HK-1212 (c/n 4987) is seen at Villavicencio in September 1997.

Luxair is the main passenger airline of the central European Grand Duchy. Boeing 737-5C9 LX-LGP (c/n 26439) is seen taking off from Palma, Majorca in September 2000. The 737 is the largest type in the fleet.

Above: The majority of the fleet of LASSA – Linea de Aeroservicios is made up of helicopters. Largest aircraft in the mixed fleet is Dornier Do 228-202 CC-CNW (c/n 8063). Its operations include flights to holiday islands off the coast of Chile. It is pictured at its Santiago-Tobalaba base in October 2003.

Below: The mosquito is a problem in Florida so each county provides methods of preventing their breeding. Spraying by helicopter or aircraft is the most successful. Douglas DC-3 N10005 (c/n 25527) of Lee County Mosquito Control District is seen at the unit base, Lehigh-Buckingham in October 1998.

Above: Landa Aviation is a small Canadian charter and air taxi company. Cessna A185F Skywagon C-GJHM (c/n 185-04203) is seen on floats with wheels at the company base, Hay River, North West Territories in May 2000.

Left: Venezuelan regional carrier LAI (Linea Aerea Industria Aerea Agricola CA) is based at Barinas and operates a fleet of five aircraft. ATR 42-230 YV-950C (c/n 397) is seen at Caracas in November 1997. (RO'B)

Loganair – Scotland's Airline now flies in British Airways livery under a franchise agreement. Prior to this, BAe 146-200 G-OLCB (c/n E2103) is seen in Loganair's colours landing at Manchester in April 1991.

Lukoil is a major Russian energy company. Pictured in its colours is Yakovlev Yak-40 RA-88297 (c/n 9530142) at Moscow-Sheremetyevo in August 1997. The aircraft is owned by Transaero Express and is in a VIP corporate fit. (JDS)

Lithuanian Airlines is the major carrier of the Baltic republic. Boeing 737-2Q8 LY-GPA (c/n 22453) is seen on a service to Frankfurt in June 1997.

Lao Aviation of Vientiane has two western-designed aircraft in their fleet mix. Pictured at Bangkok in October 1998, is ATR 72-202 RDPL-34132 (c/n 396). The balance of the fleet comprises Russian and Chinese aircraft. The carrier now operates as Lao Airlines. (RO'B)

Showing off a newer livery is Lithuanian Airlines SAAB 2000 LY-SBD (c/n 2000-023). It is seen on an early-evening service from the capital Vilnius to Frankfurt in June 1999.

LOT – Polish Airlines has now replaced all its old Russian aircraft with newer western designs. Boeing 737-45D SP-LLB (c/n 27156) is seen arriving at London-Heathrow in October 1993.

With a seat capacity of 64 the ATR 72-202 of LOT – Polish Airlines can serve many routes around northern Europe. SP-LFA (c/n 246) is pictured arriving at the gate at Frankfurt in June 1997.

Maersk Air is a Danish passenger airline. Scheduled services around Europe together with domestic routes are flown, as are holiday charters. New-generation Boeing 737-7L9 OY-MRC (c/n 28006) is seen departing Palma, Majorca in September 2000.

The Province of Montenegro is one of the few parts of the old Yugoslavia still connected to Belgrade. Fokker F.28 Fellowship 4000 YU-AOH (c/n 11184) of **Montenegro Airlines** is seen at Düsseldorf in September 1998. The carrier, based at Podgorica, has five aircraft.

Above left: Macedonia used to be part of Yugoslavia but is now an independent republic. Based in the capital, Skopje, is **MAT – Macedonian Airlines**. Boeing 737-3H9 YU-ANL (c/n 23716) is seen at Zürich in August 1998. This aircraft has since been reregistered with the 'Z3' prefix of the new country as Z3-ARF.

Above right: Dutch charter operator **Martinair** is a subsidiary of KLM. Boeing 767-31A PH-MCI (c/n 25312) is seen at Manchester in May 1998. It has extra '40 Years in the air' titles: a reference to its founding in 1958 as Martin's Air Charter.

Left: Cambodian operator **Mekong Airlines** produced one of the smartest liveries to be seen, on its single aircraft. Boeing 737-524 XU-735 (c/n 26319) is seen at Singapore-Changi in February 2003. Three months later operations were suspended but with an intention to restart.

Below: Showing off its very smart livery is **Mas Air** (Aerotransportes MAS de Carga SA) of Mexico City. Douglas DC-8-71F CC-CAX (c/n 45970) is on lease from Fast Air of Chile. The aircraft is in a cargo configuration. It is pictured at Miami in October 1998.

Miami Heat is an American basketball team. To fly players to games they have a specially marked and fitted Boeing 727-225. N8866E (c/n 20268) is seen landing at base in October 1998.

MyTravel Airways is the new operating name for British holiday charter carrier Airtours. Boeing 757-225 G-PIDS (c/n 22195) is seen about to depart the company base, Manchester in August 2004, in the new full livery.

Always a rare aircraft the Antonov An-8 is now only to be found in countries with registrations of convenience. This follows the Russian CAA's withdrawal of certification for the design. 3C-DDA (c/n OV3420) is at Sharjah, UAE in March 2000, in the colours of Mandala Air Cargo.

State-owned MIAT – Mongolian Airlines has few international services. Boeing 727-281 JU-1037 (c/n 20573) is pictured at Beijing in October 1999.

Above left: Russian cargo carrier Magdan Avia Leasing had a fleet of An-12 & IL-76 aircraft. Pictured at Sharjah, UAE in March 2000, is Ilyushin IL-76TD RA-76787 (c/n 0093495854). The following year all operations were suspended.

Above right: Operating just two DC-3s in a freight role is Majestic Air Cargo at Anchorage, Alaska. Douglas DC-3 N305SF (c/n 6208) is seen at base in May 2000.

Left: Mexicargo was a Mexico City-based freight company with a very small fleet. Boeing 707-323C XA-ABU (c/n 19585) is pictured at Tucson, Arizona in April 2003 following the suspension of services in 2000. (RO'B)

MacArthur Airlines was a small Australian operator based at Camden, New South Wales. De Havilland DH.104 Dove 5 VH-DHD (c/n 04104) is seen at Melbourne-Essendon in June 1979. Operations ceased two years later. (RO'B)

Above: **Meridiana** is an Italian regional passenger airline operating domestic and international services. BAe 146-200 I-FLRI (c/n E2220) is seen at London-Gatwick in March 1995.

Right: The country of Myanmar used to be known as Burma. They have a few international services to nearby countries. Boeing 737-82R TC-APG (c/n 29329), on lease from Pegasus of Turkey, is operated by **MAI – Myanmar Airways International**. It is seen at Singapore-Changi in May 2004. (RO'B)

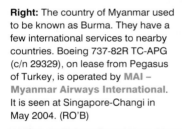

Above left: Australian carrier **Masling Commuter Services** operated a single DC-3 for charter work and newspaper deliveries. Douglas DC-3 VH-MWQ (c/n 9583) is seen at Melbourne-Essendon in December 1979. The airline had a name change to Wings Australia in 1981. (RO'B)

Above right: Pictured on the ramp at Antigua in June 1983, is de Havilland Canada DHC-6 Twin Otter 300 VP-LMD (c/n 728) of **Montserrat Air Services**. Note the luggage holder under the fuselage. The carrier suspended services in 1988. (RO'B)

Left: Looking very smart is Lockheed P2V-7 Neptune N299MA (c/n 726-7211) of **Minden Air**. The company is a water-bomber operator protecting national forests against fires. It is pictured at Avra Valley, Arizona in October 1998.

Right: Metrojet was a low-cost division of US Airways, flying domestic scheduled services. Boeing 737-201 N274US (c/n 22754) is seen arriving at Miami in October 1998. The carrier suspended operations in 2001.

Below: MEA – Middle East Airlines is based in Beirut. Services are flown to Europe, the Far East, Africa, and the Middle East. Boeing 747-2B4B N203AE (c/n 21099) is seen on approach to London-Heathrow in July 1997.

American commuter company Mesa Airlines can be found in two guises. One is operating as themselves and the other operating feeder services for four major US carriers in those carriers' livery. Canadair Regional Jet 200LR N27173 (c/n 7173) is seen at Phoenix, Arizona in October 1998, in Mesa's own markings.

Above: Taipei, Taiwan-based Mandarin Airlines is owned by China Airlines. Most of the long-haul aircraft have been merged into the parent company leaving just small domestic types for commuter operations. McDonnell Douglas MD-11 B-150 (c/n 48468) is seen at Amsterdam-Schiphol in August 1997.

Below: Based at Chicago's downtown Midway Airport, US regional carrier Midway Airlines grew in the years following deregulation. Boeing 737-2T4 N703ML (c/n 22529) is seen at Miami in June 1989. The airline ceased operations in November 1991.

Above: Malta Air Charter was a wholly owned subsidiary of Air Malta. They operated only one route, that being from Malta International Airport at Luqa to the nearby island of Gozo. A fleet of three Russian-built helicopters were used. Mil Mi-8P LZ-CAV (c/n 7411) is seen at base in September 2004. The Bulgarian-leased helicopters did not meet European Joint Aviation Regulations (JAR-OPS). Following Malta joining the EU in May 2004 the service was given notice to close, and this occurred at the end of October of that year.

Below: Russia has produced many airlines that have come and gone in a few years. Such a carrier was Mals Air Company which had just a single aircraft. Tupolev Tu-154M RA-85726 (c/n 908) is seen at its Moscow-Vnukovo base in August 1997. The following year, services were suspended. (JDS)

Luton-based **Monarch Airlines** have been flying holiday charters since 1968; they have added to this a number of scheduled services to Spanish resorts. Displaying the new company livery is Airbus A320-212 G-OZBB (c/n 389). It is pictured departing Manchester in April 2004.

Malev Hungarian Airlines have disposed of their Russian-built aircraft. Pictured arriving at Frankfurt's Terminal 2 in June 1997 is Boeing 737-4Y0 HA-LEN (c/n 26069).

Left: Malaysia Airlines is one of the leading operators of worldwide scheduled passenger services in the Far East. They are one of the few carriers to operate both the Boeing 777 and the Airbus A330 widebody twins. Boeing 777-2H6 9M-MRB (c/n 28409) is seen at Amsterdam-Schiphol in August 1997.

Right: MASkargo is the operating name for Malaysian's cargo division. It is based at Kuala Lumpur, as is the passenger division. Leased Boeing 747-230B TF-ARL (c/n 22671) is seen at Sydney-Kingsford Smith in October 2004. (RO'B)

Below: At the other end of the scale **Malaysian Airlines** operate a fleet of 39 small Boeings on domestic and regional international services. Boeing 737-4H6 9M-MQD (c/n 26461) is seen at Singapore-Changi in February 2003.

Mexicana operate flights from Mexico City. Both domestic and regional international services are flown. Airbus A320-231 F-OHMF (c/n 259) is seen approaching to land at Los Angeles-LAX in October 2001.

Right: Australian passenger carrier **Macair Airlines** has bases at both Townsville and Cairns in the northern part of Queensland. Nineteen-seat Metros make up the majority of the fleet. Seen at Brisbane-Archerfield in February 2003 is Swearingen SA-227AC Metro III VH-UZS (c/n AC-616).

Below: Iranian passenger carrier **Mahan Air** has a mixed fleet of Russian and Airbus types. Airbus A300B4-103 EP-MHE (c/n 035) is seen at its gate at Bangkok in January 2002.

Above: Established in 1982 **Manx Airlines** flew regional services from the Isle of Man. They were part of the British Regional Airlines group. BAe 4100 Jetstream 41 G-MAJA (c/n 41032) is seen at base in May 2000. The carrier was merged into British Airways Citiexpress in March 2002. (RO'B)

Below: Pictured at Newark, New Jersey in July 1970 is **Mohawk Airlines** BAC One-Eleven 204AF N2111J (c/n 029). Mohawk, based at Utica in upstate New York, was one of the first American companies to operate the type. In 1972 the carrier was acquired by Allegheny and merged into their network. (SGW)

Above: **Midwest Express** was an American regional carrier with an all DC-9 and MD-80 fleet operating from Milwaukee. McDonnell Douglas MD-81 N808ME (c/n 48070) is seen at Boston in July 1999. The carrier is now known as Midwest Airlines. (RO'B)

Right: Icelandic carrier **MD Airlines** operated a fleet of three McDonnell Douglas aircraft. MD-83 TF-MDD (c/n 49602) is at its Terminal 2 gate at Manchester in August 2003. The following year operations were suspended. (RO'B)

Above left: One of the smallest parts of the TACA group of airlines, **NICA** (Nicaraguenses de Aviacion SA) flies from Managua, the capital of Nicaragua. Boeing 737-2T5 N501NG (c/n 22395) lands at Miami in October 1998.

Above right: Montreal-based **Nationair** was a Canadian charter company with many services to Europe. Boeing 757-28A C-GNXC (c/n 24260) lands at Manchester in May 1992. The following year services were suspended.

Right: **NSW – New Southways** is a cargo sales agent that has bought space on this Taesa aircraft and so it carries joint titles. McDonnell Douglas DC-10-30F XA-TDC (c/n 46891) is seen at Miami in October 1998.

Above left: **Nouvelair** is a Tunisian charter operator based at Monastir. McDonnell Douglas MD-83 EI-CBO (c/n 49442) is seen at Düsseldorf in September 1998.

Above right: Pictured taking off from Guayaquil, Ecuador in September 1997 is Boeing 727-2M7 CC-CSW (c/n 21655) of **National Airlines (Chile) SA**. This Santiago-based carrier had a fleet of 727 and 737 airliners. At the start of 1999 they merged into Avant Airlines.

Right: **Northwest Flying** is a Canadian seasonal operator flying tourists, fishermen and hunters during the summer months. De Havilland Canada DHC-3 Otter C-GYYS (c/n 276) is at the carrier's Nestor Falls, Ontario base in June 1990.

Right: Most governments in the world have specially fitted aeroplanes to fly the head of state or other VIPs to their required locations. The size and age of the aircraft depends upon the country's wealth, status or ego. Seen on a visit to London-Heathrow in July 2002 is Boeing 727-2N6 5N-FGN (c/n 22825) operated by the **Nigerian Government**. It is of note that this VIP aircraft has been fitted with winglets.

Native American Air Ambulance is an air service whose name indicates its function. Pictured on the ramp at the company base, Williams-Gateway, Arizona in October 1998 is Pilatus PC-12 N226PC (c/n 226).

As can be seen by the livery, Italian airline **Neos** is part of the large European TUI group of carriers. Boeing 737-86N I-NEOT (c/n 33004) is seen on approach to Liverpool in September 2002.

Pictured on the ramp at Sharjah, UAE in March 2000, is Antonov An-12BP S9-BAN (c/n 402111) with **Natalco Air Lines** titles. This freighter is registered in São Tomé & Principe, a country often used as a register of convenience.

Above: British Airways leased a 747 to **Nigeria Airways** and the two airlines operated it jointly. Boeing 747-236B G-BDXB (c/n 21239) is seen at London-Heathrow in March 2000, in the colours of the Nigerian flag carrier. (SGW)

Right: One of the many airlines that came and went following the 1979 deregulation in America was **New York Air**. It was a high-frequency, low-cost operator based at La Guardia airport. Douglas DC-9-32 N535TX (c/n 47111) is seen at Boston in August 1986. Its owners, the Texas Air group, merged the carrier into Continental the following year.

Canadian carrier **Nordair** was based in Quebec. It flew regional passenger and cargo services as well as some charter work. Boeing 737-242 C-GNDM (c/n 22074) is on pushback at Toronto in July 1986. The airline was merged into Canadian the following year.

Based at the city airport, **North Vancouver Airlines** are a small commuter and air taxi company. BAe 3101 Jetstream 31 N423UE (c/n 799) is seen at base in May 2000.

Above: **Nordeste** (Linhas Aereas Regionais) is a Brazilian regional passenger carrier based in the coastal town of Salvador. Boeing 737-53A PT-MND (c/n 24786) is seen at São Paulo Domestic in October 1998. (RO'B)

Below: New York-based **North American Airlines** is a charter company specialising in the Caribbean with an all-Boeing fleet. Seen at Los Angeles in February 1999, is new-generation Boeing 737-8Q8 N800NA (c/n 28215). (RO'B)

Northern Air Cargo is the largest DC-6 operator in the world. It is based at Anchorage and carries anything needed in the state that will fit into its aircraft. Douglas DC-6BF N867TA (c/n 45202) is seen raising a dust storm at Fairbanks in May 2000. Amongst the thirteen DC-6s operated, this one and one other are swing tail conversions.

Nippon Cargo Airlines is a Japanese freight-only carrier with a fleet of fourteen 747s. Based at Tokyo-Narita, it flies regular services to Amsterdam-Schiphol, where Boeing 747-281F JA8167 (c/n 23138) is seen in October 1999.

Above: Northern Air Fuels is an associate company of NAC. It operates a flying tanker that takes various fuel oils to locations such as mining camps. Douglas DC-6A N7780B (c/n 45372) is seen at Fairbanks, Alaska in May 2000.

Left: National Airlines was a Las Vegas-based 757 operator. It flew scheduled passenger services to domestic destinations. Boeing 757-236 N544NA (c/n 29942) is seen landing at Los Angles-LAX in October 2001. In November of the following year services were suspended.

Seen outside its hangar at Minneapolis-St Paul in May 2000, is Northwest Airlink SAAB SF340A N89XJ (c/n 340A-089). The carrier provides commuter and feeder services for Northwest and is operated for them by Mesaba Airlines.

Above: Nationwide Airlines is a South African scheduled passenger carrier. Boeing 737-230 ZS-OIV (c/n 22634) is seen at Cape Town in May 2000. Note the small Sabena titles on the nose; the company operated a franchise agreement with the Belgian flag carrier. (RO'B)

Right: The BAC One-Eleven in freight conversion is a rare machine. Nationwide Cargo operates one together with its passenger-configured examples. BAC One-Eleven 409AY(F) ZS-NNM (c/n 108) is seen at Lanseria in August 2000. (RO'B)

Left: Largest aircraft in the Northwest Airlines fleet is the 747. Seen in the carrier's new livery at Tokyo-Narita in October 2004 is Boeing 747-251B N624US (c/n 21706). This particular aircraft is configured in a seat capacity of 349 in a two-class layout.

Below: Northwest Airlines of Minneapolis-St Paul is one of the largest American carriers. It operates domestic and worldwide international services. The smallest type in the fleet, only recently withdrawn, is the 'baby' DC-9 with a 78-seat capacity. Douglas DC-9-14 N8915E (c/n 45832) is seen at base in May 2000.

Northwest Jet Link Avro RJ85A N508XJ (c/n E2318) is seen at Minneapolis-St Paul in May 2000. The Jet Link carrier provides the same service as the Airlink and is also operated by Mesaba.

Above: Cargo operations continue to grow and many airlines have large numbers of dedicated freight aircraft. Northwest Cargo operates fourteen jumbos in this role. Boeing 747-249F N643NW (c/n 22245) is seen at Tokyo-Narita in October 2004. It carries extra titles 'Investing in Pacific Trade'.

American carrier Northeast was based in Boston and covered the region in the days of regulation. Douglas DC-9-31 N979NE (c/n 47097) is at Newark, New Jersey in July 1970. The airline was merged into Delta during 1972. (SGW)

Right: NAL – Nakanihon Airlines is based at Nagoya and operates feeder services for ANA. Fokker 50 JA8200 (c/n 20307) is seen at base in October 2004.

Omskavia is a Russian passenger airline with a fleet of Tu-154s and a single An-24. Based in the city of Omsk, it flies domestic operations. Tupolev Tu-154B-1 RA-85291 (c/n 291) is pictured at Moscow-Vnukovo in August 1997. (JD)

Above: O'Connor Airlines is a small South Australian carrier with a fleet of five aircraft that can provide a seating capacity from five to nineteen passengers. The company base is Mount Gambier. BAe 3201 Jetstream 32EP VH-OAE (c/n 851) is seen at Melbourne-Tullamarine in February 2003.

Below: Orient Avia was one of many short-lived Russian airlines. Founded in 1994 to fly to the far east of the country, it suspended operations in July 1997. Tupolev Tu-134A RA-65144 (c/n 60977) is seen in store at Moscow-Sheremetyevo the following month. (JDS)

Above: Orca Bay Aviation had a single 727 that was used for charters for two of Vancouver's hockey and basketball sports teams. Boeing 727-232 N7270B (c/n 20641) is seen at Seattle-Boeing Field in May 2000. Operations were suspended the following year.

Below: Based in Cumana, Venezuela, Oriental de Aviacion operated a fleet of 32-seat Russian commuter aircraft. Yakovlev Yak-40 YV-598C (c/n 9641450) is seen at Caracas in March 1998. The following year operations were suspended. (RO'B)

Left: The Greek national flag carrier is **Olympic Airways**. State-owned but up for sale, having been renamed Olympic Airlines, it operates both domestic and worldwide scheduled services. Airbus A340-313X SX-DFA (c/n 235) is seen landing at London-Heathrow in July 2002.

Below: **Olympic Aviation** is the commuter arm of Olympic Airways. Destinations served include the many Greek Islands. Shorts SH.330-100 SX-BGC (c/n SH3065) lands at Athens in June 1993.

Orient Eagle Airways was a Kazakstan-based operator with a pair of VIP-configured aircraft. Boeing 737-2H4 P4-NEN (c/n 20925) is seen at its Almaty base in February 1999. Operations were suspended in 2002. (RO'B).

Orient Thai Airlines is a growing low-cost carrier based at Bangkok. Boeing 747-238B HS-UTC (c/n 21658) is seen at Singapore-Changi in February 2003. The livery reflects that United Airlines in the USA had previously used this aircraft.

Above: Japanese commuter carrier **Orient Air Bridge** is based at Nagasaki with a fleet of five aircraft. Largest is the DHC-8-201 Dash 8-Q200. JA801B (c/n 566) is seen at base in October 2004.

Right: Based in Zürich, Swiss carrier **Odette Airways** operated a single aircraft for passenger services. McDonnell Douglas MD-83 HB-INV (c/n 49359) is seen at base in September 2004. The airline is now known as Helvetic Airways.

Used by **PIA – Pakistan International Airlines** for domestic and regional international services, the F.27 has a seating capacity of forty. Fokker F.27 Friendship 200 AP-BCZ (c/n 10305) is seen on a wet ramp at Sharjah, UAE in March 2000.

Above: Petro Produccion is the aviation division of Petro Ecuador. It flies support missions for the country's oil industry from Quito. Fairchild F-27J HC-BHD (c/n 122) is seen at base in September 1997.

Left: PIA – Pakistan International Airlines is the state-owned flag carrier. Based in Karachi it flies both domestic and worldwide scheduled passenger services. The fleet ranges from a Twin Otter to a 747. Pictured in the new livery is Boeing 777-240(ER) AP-BGJ (c/n 33775). It is seen about to depart Manchester in April 2004.

Below: Charter company **Peach Air** was set up by Caledonian Airways and Goldcrest Aviation. It operated holiday flights. Lockheed L-1011 TriStar 1 TF-ABE (c/n 1022) is seen on approach to the company base at London-Gatwick in August 1997. Services were suspended in November 1998.

Above: Pemex is the Mexican petrol and oil company. Lockheed L-100-30 Hercules XC-EXP (c/n 4851) is seen at Miami in August 1986.

Right: Named after the St Petersburg airport at which it is based, **Pulkovo Aviation Enterprise** is a passenger airline with a fleet mix of Tu-134, Tu-154 and IL-86 airliners. Pictured arriving at Frankfurt in June 1999, is Russian widebody Ilyushin IL-86 RA-86106 (c/n 51483208074).

PrivatAir is a Swiss company with a German subsidiary. It leases out Airbus and Boeing jets in various VIP seating configurations. Airbus A319-131 D-APAB (c/n 1955) is seen at Liverpool in August 2003.

Above: PSA – Pacific Southwest Airlines was based at San Diego, California. Its main route was along the Pacific coast to the cities of Los Angeles and San Francisco. Scheduled services were flown at a high frequency and with no-frills fares. BAe 146-200A N305PS (c/n E2027) is seen at Los Angeles-LAX in August 1986. Two years later the carrier was taken over by US Air.

Left: State-owned, the flag carrier of Uruguay is **PLUNA** (Primeras Lineas Aereas Uruguayas de Navigacion Aerea). Like many South American airlines it has a long history, being founded in 1936. Boeing 737-2A3 CX-BON (c/n 22737) is seen at the Uruguayan holiday resort of Punta del Este in October 2003.

Right: One of many aviation firsts that Pan American World Airways had was that of operating the first passenger 747 service. It flew the American flag worldwide from 1927 until 1991. Boeing 747-221F N905PA (c/n 21744) is operated by **Pan Am Cargo** and is seen landing at Miami in October 1981.

Below: PGA – Portugalia Airlines is a Lisbon-based regional passenger carrier with Fokker 100 and ERJ145 airliners. Seen on climb-out at Palma, Majorca in September 2000 is Embraer EMB-145EP CS-TPG (c/n 145014).

French regional carrier **Proteus Airlines** had bases at Dijon and Lyon. It operated part of its fleet as a franchise agreement with Air France; such aircraft have joint titles. Dornier Do 328-110 F-GOFB (c/n 3087) is seen at Zürich in August 1998.

Left: Pacific Air Freighters was the last Australian operator of four-engine piston-powered propliners. Douglas DC-4 VH-PAF (c/n 27352) is seen at the company base, Brisbane-Archerfield in February 2003. Later the same year, operations were suspended.

Below: Associated with Vietnam Airlines, **Pacific Airlines** is based in Ho Chi Minh City, formerly known as Saigon. They have an all-Airbus fleet. Pictured at Hong Kong in March 2003 is Airbus A321-131 S7-RGJ (c/n 604).

Above left: Phoenix Aviation is a mixed passenger and cargo airline from Kyrgyzstan but based at Sharjah, UAE. Many of the fleet have registrations in other countries. Ilyushin IL-76TD T9-CAC (c/n 0023437076) has a Bosnia-Herzegovina registration as it is jointly operated with Bio Air Company of Sarajevo. It is seen at base in March 2000.

Left: US domestic carrier **Piedmont Airlines** is one of the successes of deregulation. It expanded from its original base in North Carolina to a size that merited the name change to US Air in 1989. Boeing 737-301 N312P (c/n 23261) is seen at Dayton, Ohio in July 1986.

Below left: Operating Piedmont's commuter services was **Piedmont Commuter System**. Shorts 360 N690PC (c/n SH3690) is pictured at Charlotte, South Carolina in May 1989.

Above: Danish holiday charter company **Premiair** is owned by UK operator Airtours, hence the similar livery. Airbus A300B4-120 OY-CNL (c/n 128) departs Palma, Majorca in September 2000. As with the UK operation the carrier is now known as MyTravel Airways.

Left: Pacific Blue is the name of the offshoot of Virgin Blue operating international services from Australia. Boeing 737-8FE VH-VOO (c/n 33796) is seen at Sydney-Kingsford Smith in October 2003. (RO'B)

Above left: Pantanal (Linhas Aereas Sul-Matogrossenses SA) is a Brazilian domestic operator. They have an all-ATR fleet. ATR 42-300 PT-MFH (c/n 029) is seen at the company base, São Paulo, in January 1998. (RO'B)

Above right: Operating a fleet of four aircraft types, President Airways of Phnom Penh, Cambodia carries both passengers and cargo. Leased Antonov An-12BP RA-11301 (c/n 00347107) is at Sharjah, UAE in March 2000.

Left: Alaskan operator Pen Air have a fleet of some 40 aircraft seating from 5 to 30 passengers. Services are flown all over the state. Swearingen SA-227AC Metro III N41NE (c/n AC-741B) is seen at Anchorage in May 2000.

Above left: Based in Bangkok, PB Air is a regional passenger carrier. Fokker F.28-4000 Fellowship HS-PBC (c/n 11120) is seen at base in January 2002.

Above right: Purolator Courier is a parcel delivery company. Painted in its full livery is this Boeing 727-225F C-GKFH (c/n 20153). Kelowna Flightcraft operates it for the company. Note this 727 has been fitted with winglets. It is seen at Kelowna, British Columbia in May 2000.

Right: Many Pen Air operations are to service the remote settlements in America's largest state, Alaska. Cessna 208 Caravan 1 N9304F (c/n 208-0008) is seen at Port Heiden, one of the towns along the Aleutian chain of islands, in May 2000.

Left: Vancouver-based, **Pacific Coastal Airlines** flies a mix of types on scheduled services around the region. As well as land-based aircraft, some are on floats and some amphibians. Shorts 360 C-GPCJ (c/n SH3633) is seen at base in June 2000. (RO'B)

Below left: **Polynesian – The Airline of Samoa** is based in the capital, Apia. The fleet mix is from 9 to 154 seats. Regional international services are operated by Boeing 737-8Q8 5W-SAO (c/n 30639). It is seen at Sydney-Kingsford Smith in March 2004. (RO'B)

Below right: A mixed passenger and freight carrier, based at Johannesburg-Rand, **Phoebus Apollo Aviation** is one of South Africa's leading propliner operators. Douglas DC-3 ZS-DIW (c/n 11991) is seen at base in October 2001. (RO'B)

Above left: Pictured on climb-out from Palma, Majorca in September 2000 is Boeing 737-229 G-CEAC (c/n 20911) operated by British holiday company **Palmair**. This operator leases the aircraft from European Air Charter.

Above right: Russian operator **Perm Airlines** flies both passengers and cargo from its base in the city of Perm. Tupolev Tu-134A-3 RA-65775 (c/n 62530) is seen at Frankfurt in June 1999.

Right: The Aviation Traders ATL.98 Carvair is a Douglas DC-4 fitted with a new cargo nose. Only 21 were converted and just a couple of examples are still airworthy. 9J-PAA (c/n 21/27314) was the last built. It is seen with **Phoebus Apollo Aviation** at Rand in September 2004. (RO'B)

Above left: Formed in 1980, **PEOPLExpress** grew at such a rate it was not always able to handle the vast number of passengers that arrived at their Newark, New Jersey base. Boeing 727-243 N576PE (c/n 21269) is seen at Boston in August 1986. In February of the following year they were taken over by Continental Airlines.

Above right: **Pacific International Airlines** were a Panamanian-based cargo carrier with three 727s. Pictured at Miami in October 1998 is Boeing 727-23F HP-1229PFC (c/n 18429), their first aircraft. In 2000 the company suspended operations.

Left: **Perimeter Airlines (Inland)** is a Canadian commuter operator flying from Winnipeg, Manitoba to many locations within the region. Swearingen SA-226TC Metro II C-FHOZ (c/n TC-283) is seen at base in June 1990.

Right: **Philippine Airlines** is the national flag carrier. Pictured at Frankfurt in June 1997, is Airbus A340-211 F-OHPG (c/n 074).

Below left: Based at Karaj, Iranian cargo airline **Payam Air** has a mixed fleet. Largest type operated is the Ilyushin IL-76M. EP-TPO (c/n 063407191) is seen on the ramp at Sharjah, UAE in March 2000.

Below right: Despite its name, **Phuket Airlines** is based in the Thai capital, Bangkok. They have grown in just a few years from a single 737 to operating five Jumbos. Boeing 737-281 HS-AKO (c/n 20507) is seen on the move, at base, in January 2002.

Qantas Link is the name used by different carriers to operate feeder services for the main company, with aircraft in full livery. Boeing 717-231 VH-VQH (c/n 55094) of Impulse Airlines is seen at Melbourne-Tullamarine in February 2003. This airline has since been renamed Jetstar and is operated as a low-cost arm of Qantas.

Above: This Qantas Link BAe 146-200A VH-YAE (c/n E2107) is operated by Airlink of Perth, Western Australia. It is a franchise operation and is pictured at Melbourne-Tullamarine in February 2003.

Left: Think of Australian airlines and the name Qantas springs to mind. Once operating only long-haul services, they can now be found on domestic routes. Airbus A330-201 VH-EBA (c/n 508) is seen at Melbourne-Tullamarine in February 2003.

Below: Doha-based Qatar Airways is one of the growing Persian Gulf carriers. Airbus A300-622R A7-ABX (c/n 554) is seen at its gate at Bangkok in January 2002. The airline has an all-Airbus fleet, with the giant A380 on order.

Above left: Rusty Myers Flying Service is a Canadian floatplane operator based in northern Ontario. Seen at its Fort Francis base is de Havilland Canada DHC-2 Beaver C-FOBY (c/n 13) in June 1990.

Above right: Based at Ciudad Bolivar in central Venezuela, RUTACA (Rutas Aereas CA) flies a mixed fleet, from a single-engine Cessna to a 737. PZL-Mielec An-2 YV-205C (c/n IG185-58) is at base in November 1992. This aircraft is a Polish-built example of the well-known Russian design.

Left: Flag carrier for the Hashemite Kingdom of Jordan is Royal Jordanian. Services are flown both east and west of its Amman base. Lockheed L-1011 TriStar 500 JY-AGD (c/n 1229) is seen at Amsterdam-Schiphol in August 1997.

Above left: Royal Brunei Airlines is the sole scheduled passenger carrier in the oil-rich state. Airbus A319-132 V8-RBR (c/n 2032) is seen at Singapore-Changi in August 2004. (RO'B)

Above right: Pictured at Moscow-Zhukovsky in August 1995, is Russian Government Antonov An-124-100 Ruslan RA-82072 (c/n 9773053359136). This heavy-lift cargo aircraft would be used to transport such items as special automobiles for use by the Russian President on foreign trips.

Right: REX – Regional Express is an Australian commuter based at Wagga Wagga. Pictured at Bathurst in February 2003 is SAAB 340B VH-SBA (c/n 340B-311).

A subsidiary of Varig, **RIO-SUL** (Servicos Aereos Regionais SA) is a Rio-based regional passenger airline. Fokker 50 PT-SRA (c/n 20261) is seen at São Paulo in January 1998. (RO'B)

State-owned **Royal Nepal Airlines** is based at Kathmandu. Services include domestic, Far Eastern and European. Boeing 757-2F8 9N-ACB (c/n 23863) is seen at Frankfurt in June 1999.

Founded in 1979 following a merger, **Republic Airlines** was based at Minneapolis-St Paul. Boeing 727-2M7 N725RW (c/n 21502) is seen at Boston in August 1986. The company was taken over by Northwest Airlines in the same year.

Above: Canadian floatplane operator **Red Lake Airways** operates summer-only services to lakeside lodges in northern Ontario. Noorduyn Norseman V C-FJIN (c/n CCF-55) is seen at Red Lake Sea Plane Base in June 1990.

Left: **Rich International** operated cargo services and, later, passenger charters. Douglas DC-8-62 N1808E (c/n 46105) is pictured at Boston in August 1986. The airline ceased operations in 1997.

Below left: **Reeve Aleutian** was one of the lifeline operators in Alaska. They flew cargo and passengers to many remote locations. Lockheed L-188C Electra N1968R (c/n 2007) is seen landing in late-evening sunshine at its Anchorage base in May 2000. These aircraft are operated in a combi role. They were the last company to fly passengers in the Electra and in March 2001 the airline ceased operations.

South African carrier **Rovos Air** flies passengers in three vintage propliners. Convair CV-440 ZS-ARV (c/n 228) is seen at its base of Pretoria-Wonderboom in September 2004. (RO'B)

Left: Ryanair of Dublin is one of Europe's largest low-cost no-frills carriers with passenger flights to many European cities. EI-DAM is a new-generation Boeing 737-8AS (c/n 33719). It is pictured landing at Stansted in August 2003. The airline operates many flights from this location.

Below: One of the most famous aviation services in the world is that of the **Royal Flying Doctor Service** of Australia. Based in Sydney they have aircraft deployed all around that vast country. Beech King Air B200 VH-MWU (c/n BB-1418) is seen at Melbourne-Essendon in February 2003.

RAM – Royal Air Maroc is the state-owned airline of Morocco. The fleet is overwhelmingly Boeings with 737, 747, 757 and 767 types being flown. Boeing 757-2B6 CN-RMT (c/n 23686) is seen at Frankfurt in June 2001.

Region Air of Singapore could not be accused of having a lavish livery. Their name is in small letters, just aft of the forward door. Airbus A320-212 S7-RGL (c/n 542) is seen at its Changi base in February 2003. Later that year services were suspended.

Above: RAC – Ryukyu Air Commuter is based on the Japanese island of Okinawa. They operate services to the surrounding smaller islands. Pilatus Britten-Norman BN-2B Islander JA5325 (c/n 2298) is seen at base in October 2004.

Right: An Air France subsidiary, **Regional Airlines** is based at Nantes. It flies scheduled passenger services around Europe. Some aircraft operate under a franchise operation for their parent company in its livery. ATR 42-300 F-GEQJ (c/n 008) is seen at Geneva in May 1997 in the subsidiary's colours. (JDS)

Above: British airline **Scillonia Airways** operated Rapides from Land's End to the Scilly Isles. De Havilland DH.89A Dragon Rapide G-AJCL (c/n 6722) is seen at East Midlands in April 1968. The carrier went into liquidation later that year. (SGW)

Below: There are few VIP-equipped C-130s. One such is operated by the **Saudi Arabian Royal Flight**, a division of Saudia Arabian Airlines. The fleet ranges from a Learjet to a Jumbo. Lockheed 382C (VC-130H) Hercules HZ-114 (c/n 4E-4843) is seen at Stansted in July 1998. (SGW)

Swissair Asia was the company set up by Swissair to operate services to Taiwan without upsetting the government in Beijing. McDonnell Douglas MD-11 HB-IWN (c/n 48539) is seen at Bangkok in November 1999. Note the different tail logo in place of the white cross.

The short-body Boeing 747SP has found a new lease of life as a head-of-state VIP private jet. It has both a very long range and a large amount of space. Boeing 747SP-68 HZ-AIF (c/n 22503) is operated by the **Saudi Arabian Royal Flight**. It is seen landing at Stansted in August 2003.

Jeddah-based **Saudi Arabian Airlines** have a huge fleet of very new Boeing and Airbus types. Showing the new livery at Frankfurt in June 1999 is Boeing 777-268 HZ-AKF (c/n 28349).

Above: **Swissair** was one of the best-known and respected airlines in the world. Services were flown both domestic and worldwide. McDonnell Douglas MD-11 HB-IWL (c/n 48456) climbs out of Runway 16 at Zürich in August 1998. It came as a great surprise to many when they ceased operations in March 2002.

Left: **Swiss International Air Lines** is the successor to Swissair and emerged following a takeover by Crossair. Embraer RJ145LU HB-JAY (c/n 145601) is seen in the new livery at Manchester in April 2004.

Long-haul flights for **Swiss** are operated by the four-engine twin-aisle Airbus. Pictured at its Zürich base, in September 2004, is Airbus A340-313 HB-JMD (c/n 556).

Swiss operates a wide variety of both single- and twin-aisle Airbus aircraft. The range is A319, 320, 321, 330 and 340. Seen departing its Zürich base, in September 2004, is Airbus A330-223 HB-IQJ (c/n 294).

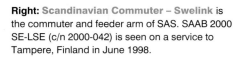

Above left: A subsidiary of Singapore Airlines, **Silk Air** operates an all-Airbus fleet. Pictured at its Changi base in February 2003 is Airbus A319-132 9V-SBD (c/n 1698).

Above right: SN Brussels Airlines is the Belgian carrier that has taken over many of the Sabena routes; it evolved from DAT. Avro RJ100 OO-DWB (c/n E3315) is seen at Manchester in June 2002.

Right: Scandinavian Commuter – Swelink is the commuter and feeder arm of SAS. SAAB 2000 SE-LSE (c/n 2000-042) is seen on a service to Tampere, Finland in June 1998.

Sis-Q Flying Services used to be a California-based water-bomber operator. Douglas DC-6B N888SQ (c/n 43562) is seen on station at Wenatchee-Pangborn, Washington state in September 1984. Following a name change to Macavia, water-bomber operations were run down.

SABENA (Société Anonyme Belge d'Exploitation de la Navigation Aérienne) had a long history dating back to 1923. It was a sad day in November 2001 when an airline with a 78-year history ceased operations. Airbus A340-211 OO-SCW (c/n 014) is seen landing at Zürich in August 1998.

Right: Operating the high-performance Antonov An-32 is **SEAP** (Servicios Aereos Especializados en Transportes Petroleros SA). As its name suggests it supports the Colombian oil industry. HK-4011X (c/n 3208) is seen at its Bogota base in September 1997.

Below: Iranian airline **Saha Air** is linked to that nation's air force. It flies both passenger and cargo operations. Boeing 707-3J9C EP-SHE (c/n 21128) is seen landing at Dubai in March 1997.

Sunbird is an Icelandic tour company. Operating Boeing 737-3Q8 TF-FDA (c/n 24700) on their behalf is Icelandic airline Islandsflug. It is pictured departing Palma, Majorca in September 2000, on a holiday charter flight.

American commuter company **SkyWest Airlines** fleet can be seen in the livery of several major airlines, as it provides feeder services for Delta, Continental and United. Swearingen SA-226TC Metro II N161SW (c/n TC-293) is at Santa Barbara, California in September 1988 in SkyWest's own colours.

Above: Istanbul-based **Sunways** (Intersun Havacilik AS) was a Turkish holiday charter company. Boeing 757-23A SE-DSM (c/n 24528) lands at Dubai in March 1997. Six months later operations were suspended.

Right: **Southern Air Transport** was a Miami-based all-cargo operation flying charters worldwide. Douglas DC-8-73F N875SJ (c/n 46063) is at Sharjah, UAE in March 1997. Operations were suspended in September of the following year.

Venezuelan passenger carrier **Servivensa** (Servicios Avensa SA) is a subsidiary of Avensa. Boeing 727-22 YV-763C (c/n 18327) is seen at its Caracas base in November 1992. The livery of this carrier has a wonderful 1950s style that still looks good today.

Above: **Sayakhat** is an Almaty, Kazakstan-based passenger and cargo airline. The former fly in Tu-154s and the latter in IL-76s. Pictured on the cargo ramp at Urumqi, China is Ilyushin IL-76TD UN-76385 (c/n 1033416515) in October 1999.

Left: Most Chinese airlines have abandoned their Soviet-built aircraft. One of the last operators of the Tupolev Tu-154M was **Sichuan Airlines** of Chengdu. B-2629 (c/n 919) is seen on touchdown at Guangzhou in October 1999.

Below: Canadian backwoods operator **Sabourin Lake Airways** was based at Cochenour, Ontario. It flew a mixture of float- and landplane operations. Flying over Sabourin Lake Sea Plane Base in June 1990, is Noorduyn Norseman VI C-FJEC (c/n 469). The carrier suspended services in 1996.

Tupolev Tu-154M RA-85676 (c/n 836) is operated by another Siberian airline. This one is **Sibaviatrans** of Krasnoyarsk. It is a much smaller operation than Sibir having only a small number of jet airliners amongst a fleet of cargo and corporate aircraft. It is seen at Frankfurt in June 1999.

Sibir Airlines is a Siberian carrier with mixed cargo/passenger aircraft and roles. Seen at Frankfurt in June 1997, is Tupolev Tu-154M RA-85699 (c/n 874).

Moscow-Zhukovsky-based Antonov An-74 RA-74029 (c/n 36547097940) is operated by the **State Unitary Air Enterprise of the Ministry for Emergency Situations**. This mouthful boils down to providing state aid as and when required. They were associated with the 'Space Centre Airline' Alis at one time. The aircraft is pictured at base in August 1995.

Sky Airline is a Chilean passenger carrier with a fleet of eight first-generation 737s. Pictured on the ramp of its Santiago base in October 2003 is Boeing 737-2H6 CC-CTD (c/n 20586).

Based in Luanda, Angola, Savanair was a small cargo line with a pair of An-12s. Pictured on the ramp at Sharjah, UAE in March 2000, is Antonov An-12BP D2-FBY (c/n 8345510). The carrier suspended operations in 2002.

Above: Southern Air is an American freight carrier with a small fleet of Jumbos. Boeing 747-230B(SF) N742SA (c/n 22669) is seen at Frankfurt in June 2001.

Below: Despite its name Shortstop Jet Charter operates this 1945-vintage DC-3 for pleasure flights. Seen on the ramp, in February 2003, at its Melbourne-Essendon base is Douglas DC-3 VH-OVM (c/n 33092).

South African company Speed Services Courier operates this turbo-converted Douglas DC-3 ZS-MFY (c/n 12073). It is owned by Airworld of Pretoria-Wonderboom and was pictured at base in August 2000. (RO'B)

Above: Portuguese operator SATA International has a mixed fleet of 737 and A310 airliners at their Lisbon base. Boeing 737-4Y0 CS-TGW (c/n 23981) is seen at Frankfurt's Terminal 2 in June 2001.

Left: One thing that the many new Russian airlines do well is to choose excellent liveries for their aircraft. Tupolev Tu-154M RA-85817 (c/n 1007) is at Moscow-Domodedovo in August 1997. The operator is Samara Airlines from the city of that name. (JDS)

French holiday charter line **Star Airlines** has a fleet of wide- and narrow-body Airbus aircraft. Airbus A320-214 F-GRSH (c/n 749) is seen taking off from Palma, Majorca in September 2000.

American charter company **Sun Country Airlines** flies a fleet of new-generation 737s from its base at Minneapolis-St Paul. Seen landing at Los Angeles-LAX, in October 2001, is Boeing 737-8Q8 N800SY (c/n 30627).

Above left: Based at Medellin, Colombia, **SAM** (Sociedad Aeronautica de Medellin Consolidada SA) is a domestic carrier owned by Avianca. Avro RJ100 N512MM (c/n E3263) is seen at Bogota in September 1997.

Above right: **Skyways** is a Swedish commuter operator with European services. The fleet mix is SF340s, RJ145s, F50s and 146s. Photographed at Manchester, in August 2002, is Embraer RJ145EP SE-DZD (c/n 145185).

Left: Peruvian carrier **Star Up** operates an all-Russian built fleet of both passenger and freight aircraft. Antonov An-24RV OB-1769 (c/n 57310110) is seen at its Lima base in October 2003.

Below: Czech operator **Smart Wings** is a new low-cost operator based at Prague. Boeing 737-530 OK-SWY (c/n 24815) is seen in its distinctive livery at Zürich in September 2004.

Above: Chinese carrier **Shanghai Airlines** operates 737, 757, and 767 airliners on its major route network. It was formed in 1985 by the local government of the city as well as local investors. Boeing 757-26D B-2843 (c/n 27681) is seen at base in October 1999.

The colourful markings of **Shanghai Airlines** display the tall tail of the new-generation 737. Boeing 737-7Q8 B-2997 (c/n 28223) is pictured on a domestic flight to Guangzhou in October 1999.

Below: **SAN – Servicios Aereos Nacionales SA** is an Ecuadorian passenger carrier with a single aircraft. Boeing 727-95 HC-BJL (c/n 19596) is seen at base, Guayaquil in September 1997. The airline, a subsidiary of SAETA – Air Ecuador, ceased operations in February 2000 with the intention of restarting.

Above: **Sabre Airways** was a UK holiday charter company. It flew from a number of British airports to European resorts. Boeing 737-8Q8 G-OJSW (c/n 28218) is seen on approach to Manchester in May 1999. The carrier changed its name to Excel Airways in January 2001.

Left: **SATENA** (Servicio de Aeronavegacion a Territorios Nacionales) is the commercial arm of the Colombian Air Force. Its role is to provide an air service to locations that might not be viable for a commercial company. Fokker F.28 Fellowship 3000C FAC-1141 (c/n 11162) is pictured at Villavicencio in September 1997.

Based in the city of Saratov, Russian airline **Saravia** flies domestic services. Yakovlev Yak-42 RA-42316 (c/n 4520422202030) is seen at Moscow-Domodedovo in August 1997. (JDS)

Colombian cargo carrier **SADELCA** (Sociedad Aerea del Caqueta) operated Antonov An-32Bs for several years before reverting back to the DC-3. HK-4117X (c/n 2909) is seen at its Villavicencio base in September 1997.

The livery of Spanish holiday charter airline **Spantax** was a well known sight at European airports. Douglas DC-7C EC-BBT (c/n 45553) is seen on the move at Geneva in July 1970. The carrier had started operations in 1959 and ceased flying in 1988.

Above: **SNA – Skynet Asia Airways** is a small Japanese passenger carrier with a fleet of five 737s. It is based at Miyazaki. Boeing 737-4Y0 JA737E (c/n 26069) is seen departing Tokyo-Haneda in October 2004.

Right: **Skyservice Airlines** is a Canadian holiday charter operator flying both long- and short-haul services. Airbus A320-231 C-FTDF (c/n 437) is seen landing at Liverpool in August 2002.

Below: **Skyways of London** was part of the Skyways Coach-Air Group. This British airline was one of the first to operate holiday flights. Hawker Siddeley (Avro) 748 Srs.1-101 G-ARMW (c/n 1537) is seen at its Lympne, Kent base in May 1970.

Above: American charter carrier **Sky Trek International Airlines** operated an all-727 fleet of six aircraft from Newark, New Jersey. Boeing 727-251 N259US (c/n 19978) is seen landing at Miami in October 1998. The carrier now operates as Discovery Airlines.

Below: Honduran airline **SAHSA** (Servicio Aereo de Honduras SA) operated from the capital Tegucigalpa. Services were flown around Central America and to the USA. Boeing 737-214 HR-SHG (c/n 19921) is seen at Miami in June 1989. The carrier suspended services in January 1994.

Founded in 1994 by the local provincial government, **Shandong Airlines** is a domestic carrier based at Jinan. Boeing 737-35N B-2996 (c/n 29316) is seen at Guangzhou in October 1999.

Sharjah, UAE-based Santa Cruz Imperial Airlines had most of its cargo fleet registered in Liberia. Antonov An-12 EL-ALJ (c/n 8346202) is seen at base in March 2000. The company changed its name to Flying Dolphin Airlines.

Above: Shandong Airlines also operates commuter services around eastern China. SAAB 340B B-3657 (c/n 340B-357) is seen at Xian in October 1999.

Right: Largest aircraft in the Syrianair fleet is the Boeing 747SP-94. Configured for 324 passengers in two classes, YK-AHA (c/n 21174) is seen climbing out of Sharjah, UAE in March 2000.

Above left: Syrianair – Syrian Arab Airlines is 100% state-owned and the only carrier in the country. Tupolev Tu-154M YK-AIA (c/n 708) is seen at Moscow-Sheremetyevo in September 1995.

Above right: Spanair is a large Spanish holiday charter and scheduled carrier. McDonnell Douglas MD-83 EC-GBA (c/n 49626) is seen on approach to the company base in Palma, Majorca in September 2000.

Left: The national flag-carrier, SriLankan Airlines has an all-Airbus fleet of both wide- and narrow-body types. Airbus A330-243 4R-ALB (c/n 306) is seen climbing out of Singapore-Changi in February 2003.

Tucson-based **Sun Pacific** was an American charter airline using 727s. Boeing 727-231 N64319 (c/n 20052) is seen at base in October 1998. Operations were suspended the following April with the intention to restart.

Above: **Sunshine Express Airlines** is an Australian commuter carrier based in Queensland. Shorts SD.360-300 VH-SEG (c/n SH.3760) is seen at Brisbane in February 2003.

Left: **STAF** (Servicios de Transportes Aereos Fueguinos SA) is an Argentine passenger and cargo line that leases aircraft as required. McDonnell Douglas MD-11CF N276WA (c/n 48632) lines up to take off at Miami in October 1998. It is configured for cargo services.

Above: **Skyway Enterprises** is an American cargo company with Learjet and Shorts aircraft. Seen landing at Miami in October 1998 is Shorts SD.360-100 N367MQ (SH.3640).

Below: Chinese carrier **Shenzhen Airlines** has an all-737 fleet. Its main operations are in the south of the country providing a service to the Shenzhen special economic zone. Boeing 737-3K9 B-2933 (c/n 25788) is seen arriving at its gate at Beijing in October 1999.

Sobelair, as can be seen by the livery, was a subsidiary of Sabena. It operated the charter operations including holiday flights. Boeing 767-328 OO-STF (c/n 27212) is seen at Zürich in August 1998. The carrier survived longer than their parent but suspended operations in January 2004.

National flag carrier **Sudan Airways** still operate 707s in both cargo and passenger configuration. Boeing 707-3J8C ST-AFB (c/n 20898) is in the former role at Sharjah, UAE in March 2000.

Sud Aerocargo was a Moldovan freight carrier based at Cahul. Ilyushin IL-18D ER-ICM (c/n 182004804) is seen at Sharjah, UAE in March 2000. This aircraft represents half of the airline's fleet; an Antonov An-12 is the other. The following year operations were suspended.

Dutch carrier Schreiner Airways has a history dating back to 1945. Both passengers and freight have been carried. Airbus A300B4-203F PH-SFM (c/n 274) is seen in a cargo configuration at Amsterdam in May 2001.

Above: Slovak Airlines was founded in 1997 to fly scheduled and charter services from Bratislava. Tupolev Tu-154M OM-AAA (c/n 1014) is seen at Palma, Majorca in September 2000.

Below: SAETA – Air Ecuador is based at Quito. It operates both regional and international services. Airbus A310-304 HC-BSF (c/n 661) is pictured at Miami in April 1994. In February 2000 the carrier suspended operations with the intention to restart.

Left: American carrier Sierra Pacific Airlines has been flying passengers since 1976, with turboprops initially, now with 737s. De Havilland Canada DHC-6 Twin Otter 300 N361V (c/n 361) is seen at Marana, Arizona in October 1979.

Below left: Springbok Classic Air of Johannesburg-Rand operates a fleet of propliners. Roles include safaris to South Africa's game parks. Douglas DC-3 ZS-GPL (c/n 9581) is seen at base in September 2004. (RO'B)

Below right: SAL Express is an African freight company from São Tomé. Beech 1900C-1 Airliner S9-CAE (c/n UC-142) is seen at Lanseria in South Africa in December 1999. (RO'B)

South African Historic Flight operates a selection of types that the national carrier has flown in years past. Douglas DC-4 Skymaster ZS-AUB (c/n 42984) is pictured at its base, Pretoria-Swartkop, in September 2004. (RO'B)

The 737 has never been the most common freight aircraft. Seen at Durban in November 1998, is Boeing 737-244F ZS-SIF (c/n 22585) of South African Cargo. (RO'B)

Left: South African Airways has expanded its route network following the change of power in the country. It has also added a new livery. Boeing 747-344 ZS-SAT (c/n 22970) is seen at London-Heathrow in July 1997.

Right: South African Airlink is the commuter and feeder arm of the national carrier with aircraft in full livery. Embraer RJ135LR ZS-OTM (c/n 145485) is seen at Cape Town in April 2003. (RO'B)

Below: In America most of the large sports teams playing basketball, baseball and football charter aircraft with a special interior configured to cater for the height or girth of the players. Sports Jet is a Phoenix, Arizona-based company with a pair of Boeings. Seen at Minneapolis-St Paul in May 2000 is Boeing 737-408 N737DX (c/n 24804) with a 72-seat interior.

Sterling European Airlines of Copenhagen is a charter line with a livery to match its role. Aircraft each have a different fuselage colour and a beach-ball on the fin. Boeing 737-85H OY-SEI (c/n 29445) is seen arriving at Palma, Majorca in September 2000.

Left: Singapore Airlines are renowned for their new aircraft and unmatched cabin service. The fleet are all twin-aisle Boeing or Airbus designs. They currently operate the longest non-stop regular scheduled flight. This is an eighteen-hour trip from the Singapore-Changi base of the airline to New York. The distance is 8965nm (16,600km). Specially configured Airbus A340-541s operate the flights. 9V-SGE (c/n 563) is seen at base in October 2004. (RO'B)

Below: 'Mega Ark' is the fleet name for the Singapore Airlines Cargo Jumbos. Boeing 747-412F 9V-SFG (c/n 26558) arrives at Sharjah, UAE in March 2000. The carrier became a separate operating company in April 2001.

Above: Seen at Bangkok in November 1999, is Singapore Airlines Boeing 777-312 9V-SYB (c/n 28516). This aircraft is the stretched version of the type. In a three-class configuration it holds 332 passengers against 288 in the '200' series.

Below: American charter operator Sunworld International Airlines started services in July 1996. The fleet comprises three 727s. Photographed at Orlando, Florida in April 1999 is Boeing 727-251 N282US (c/n 21161). (JDS)

SAS – Scandinavian Airline System is one of several multi-nation airlines. It covers Denmark, Norway and Sweden. New-generation Boeing 737-883 SE-DTY (c/n 30193) climbs out of Palma, Majorca in September 2000.

Above: SAS Commuter is the feeder arm for the main carrier. DHC-8-402 Dash-8 Q400 LN-RDT (c/n 4038) is pictured at Zürich in September 2004.

Left: Seaboard World Airlines took its name in 1961 having operated since 1947 as Seaboard and Western. The New York-based company flew both charter and scheduled cargo operations. Boeing 707-345C N7321S (c/n 19840) is seen at Munich-Riem in July 1968. The carrier was taken over by Flying Tiger in 1980. (SGW)

Right: Based at Billund in Denmark, **Sun-Air of Scandinavia** operates scheduled passenger flights under a franchise agreement with British Airways. The aircraft are in BA livery. BAe 4100 Jetstream 41 OY-SVS (c/n 41014) is seen at Manchester in August 2002.

Below: **Southern Winds** is an Argentine passenger carrier with an all-Boeing fleet. Seen at the carrier's base, Buenos Aires-Aeroparque J Newbery in October 2003, is Boeing 737-205 LV-ZZA (c/n 21219).

Above: **Safair** is a South African charter company based at Johannesburg. It has a mixed fleet of passenger and cargo aircraft. Lockheed L-100-30 Hercules ZS-RSI (c/n 31C-4600) is configured for cargo at Manchester in March 2003.

Below: Based at Tokyo-Haneda, **Skymark Airlines** is owned by the HIS Travel Group. It has a fleet of five 767s. Pictured at base, in October 2004, is Boeing 767-36N(ER) JA767D (c/n 300847).

Above: Flying the Australian-built GAF N22 Nomad is **Seair Pacific Gold Coast**. VH-MSF (c/n N22B-69) is pictured at the company base of Coolangatta, Queensland in February 2003.

Right: **Styrian Spirit** is a Graz-based, Austrian carrier with a fleet of Regional Jets. Pictured at Zürich, in September 2004, is Canadair CRJ 200LR OE-LSC (c/n 7299).

Above left: TWA – Trans World Airlines was one of the oldest of the US major carriers, dating back to 1930 when it was known as Transcontinental and Western. Boeing 717-231 N402TW (c/n 55069) is seen at Minneapolis-St Paul in May 2000, in the latest livery. The carrier was taken over by American Airlines in February 2001.

Above right: TANS (Transportes Aereos Nacionales de la Selva) is a division of the Peruvian Air Force. It operates an all-737 fleet from Lima. Seen at base in October 2003 is Boeing 737-244 OB-1713 (c/n 19707).

Right: Transjet Airways was a Swedish holiday charter company. Its largest aircraft was the Jumbo, in an all-economy seating configuration. Boeing 747-212B SE-RBH (c/n 21316) is seen at Manchester in June 2002. The following month services were suspended.

Above left: Travel City Direct is a British holiday company who have leased an Air Atlanta Iceland Jumbo and painted it in their own livery. Seen at Manchester, in July 2004, is Boeing 747-267B TF-ABP (c/n 22429).

Above right: TACA International Airlines is the airline of El Salvador. It is also now a group of Central American carriers. BAC One-Eleven 407AW YS-18C (c/n 106) is seen at Miami in October 1981.

Right: Austrian regional commuter company Tyrolean Airways is based at Innsbruck and owned by Austrian Airlines. Fokker 70 OE-LFL (c/n 11573) is seen arriving at Palma, Majorca in September 2000. The fleet is being re-branded as Austrian Arrows.

Right: Thomson.co.uk is the new brand name for Britannia Airways. The parent company is the Thomson Travel Group. Boeing 767-304(ER) G-OBYE (c/n 28979) is seen departing Manchester in August 2004.

Tunisair is the national airline of Tunisia. It has a mixed Boeing and Airbus fleet. Boeing 737-5H3 TS-IOI (c/n 27257) is pictured at Düsseldorf in September 1998.

Detroit-based Trans Continental Airlines is an all-freight carrier working especially with the local motor industry. Convair CV-440 N323CF (c/n 323) is seen at Detroit-Willow Run in June 1990. The company was renamed Express.net Airlines in March 2000.

Based at Taipei, Taiwan is Chinese carrier TransAsia Airways. They fly domestic and regional international passenger services. Airbus A321-131 B-22606 (c/n 731) is seen at Macau in February 2003.

Above: Dutch charter operator Transavia Airlines is a subsidiary of KLM. As well as operating single charter flights it often leases out aircraft for short periods. New-generation Boeing 737-7K2 PH-XRA (c/n 30784) is seen on approach to Madrid in September 2002.

Right: TAROM – Romanian Air Transport has disposed of its Soviet equipment. Pictured at London-Heathrow in August 1991, is Romanian-assembled ROMBAC One-Eleven 516RC YR-BRA (c/n 401).

Russian carrier **Transaero Express** is a sister company of Transaero. Tupolev Tu-134A RA-65830 (c/n 12093) is seen at base, Moscow-Sheremetyevo, in August 1997. (JDS)

Above: Istanbul-based **Turkish Airlines** is state-owned. Services are flown to many parts of the world. Airbus A320-231 EI-TLG (c/n 428) is seen at Amsterdam-Schiphol in August 1997.

Left: The former Soviet republic of Turkmenistan has a single airline for domestic, freight and international services. Boeing 757-22K EZ-A014 (c/n 30863) of **Turkmenistan Airlines** is seen as it lines up to depart from Manchester in August 2002.

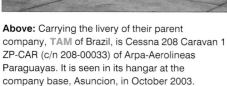

Thai Cargo operated this leased Boeing 747-2D7B N522MC (c/n 21783). It is seen landing at Frankfurt in June 1999. All of Thai Airways' own 747s are '400' series models and configured for passengers.

Above: Carrying the livery of their parent company, **TAM** of Brazil, is Cessna 208 Caravan 1 ZP-CAR (c/n 208-00033) of Arpa-Aerolineas Paraguayas. It is seen in its hangar at the company base, Asuncion, in October 2003.

Right: **Thai Airways International** is well known for their excellent cabin service. It flies both the 777 and the A330. Pictured at their Bangkok base, in November 1999, is Airbus A330-321 HS-TEC (c/n 062).

Left: Thai Airways domestic commuter services are flown by ATR 72-201 aircraft. HS-TRB (c/n 167) is pictured at Bangkok in November 1999.

Below: T doble A (Transportes Aereos Andahuaylas SA) was a small Peruvian passenger carrier, based at Cuzco, with a Yak-40 and an An-24. Pictured on its way to take-off at Lima, in September 1997, is Antonov An-24RV OB-1651 (c/n 27308303). The carrier suspended operations in 2000.

Russian airline **Tatneftaero** had a single aircraft. It was based at Kazan in the internal Republic of Tatarstan. Tupolev Tu-154M RA-85798 (c/n 982) is at Sharjah, UAE in March 2000 in the carrier's very smart livery. The following year services were suspended.

Translift Airways was an Irish holiday charter company. It operated both wide- and narrow-body Airbus aircraft. Airbus A320-231 EI-TLG (c/n 428) is seen at the airline's Dublin base in June 1994. The carrier was renamed TransAer in May 1997.

Above: Following the name change to **TransAer International Airlines** a revised livery was applied. EI-TLK Airbus A300B4-203 (c/n 158) is seen on pushback from Terminal 1 at Manchester in May 1998. In October 2000 all operations ceased and the carrier went into receivership.

Right: TAME (Linea Aerea del Ecuador) is the commercial arm of the Ecuadorean Air Force. It operates services to locations that do not always appeal to commercial carriers. Boeing 727-2T3 HC-BHM/ FAE 078 (c/n 22078) is seen at its Quito base in September 1997.

Worldwide parcel delivery company **TNT** has aircraft at many locations for its needs. Boeing 727-287F OY-SEW (c/n 21688) is seen in very late evening sunlight at Helsinki in June 1998. This aircraft is owned and operated by Sterling for TNT flights.

Above: TAN (Transportes Aereos Nacionales) was the airline for the Central American republic of Honduras. Lockheed L-188A Electra HR-TNL (c/n 1134) is pictured climbing out of Miami in October 1981. The company merged and took the name SAHSA in 1991.

Left: Operating an all-Boeing fleet from São Paulo, **Transbrasil** provided domestic and international scheduled passenger flights. Boeing 767-2B1 PT-TAK (c/n 25421) is seen at Amsterdam-Schiphol in August 1997. Operations were suspended in December 2001.

Russian transport aircraft are very popular in Peru. **TAA (Transportes Aeros Ancahuatas)** Antonov An-24B N93110 (c/n 97305501) is seen on the Police ramp at Lima in October 2003.

Titan Airways is a UK charter company based at Stansted specialising in very short-notice sub-charters. Boeing 737-33A G-ZAPM (c/n 27285) departs Palma, Majorca in September 2000. It shows the company's very distinctive markings.

Canadian operator **Tundra Helicopters** is based at Langley, British Columbia. Sikorsky S-58ET C-GHOS (c/n 58-1537) is seen at base in May 2000. The carrier has a fleet of three aircraft of two different types.

An all-Piper operator, **Tanana Air Service** has only two twin-engined aircraft in the fleet of fourteen. Piper PA-31-310 Navajo N101LJ (c/n 31-267) is seen at the company base of Fairbanks, Alaska in May 2000.

Formerly LAPSA – Air Paraguay, **TAM (Transportes Aereos del Mercosur)** is a member of the TAM group of Brazil. It operates flights from Paraguay with aircraft leased from the parent company. Fokker 100 PT-MRB (c/n 11285) is seen at a wet Asuncion in October 2003.

Above: Tweedsmuir Air Service is a Canadian floatplane operator from Nimpo Lake, British Columbia. It flies summer schedules to lodges and camps on local lakes. De Havilland Canada DHC-2 Beaver 1 C-GNPO (c/n 773) is seen in winter store at Vancouver in May 2000.

Left: Moscow-Sheremetyevo-based Transaero Airlines was one of the first Russian carriers to operate mainly Western-built aircraft. McDonnell Douglas DC-10-30 N140AA (c/n 46712) is pictured at base in August 1997. (JDS)

Below: Transwede Airways was a Swedish scheduled carrier and sister company to Transwede Leisure, based at Stockholm. Fokker 100 SE-DUC (c/n 11324) is seen at London-Gatwick in March 1995. The airline was renamed Braathens Sverige in 1998.

Above: Bangkok-based Thai Flying Service operated a single 707 freighter amongst a fleet of light twins. Boeing 707-321C HS-TFS (c/n 19372) is pictured on the ramp at Sharjah, UAE in March 2000.

Right: Trans States Airlines is a St Louis-based commuter company with franchise and code share agreements with a number of major US carriers. These include American Airlines and US Air. BAe 3201 Jetstream 32 N972JX (c/n 972) is seen at Los Angeles in February 1999. (RO'B)

Above left: Operating scheduled passenger services; **TAM Brasil** (Transportes Aereos Regionais) is based at São Paulo. PT-LAK Fokker F.27 Friendship 500 (c/n 10634) is seen at base in October 1998. (RO'B)

Above right: **TTA – Trans Travel Airlines** was a Dutch commuter company based at Lelystad. De Havilland Canada DHC-8 Dash 8-102 PH-TTA (c/n 237) is seen on a charter to Fairford in July 1997. They later operated as Cityconnect.

Left: The former Soviet republic of Kazakstan has spawned a large number of airlines. **TAA – Trans Asia Airlines** was based at Almaty with three IL-62s. Ilyushin IL-62M UN-86501 (c/n 4831628) is seen landing at Frankfurt in June 1999. Later that year services were suspended with the intention to restart.

Above left: **Titan Cargo** was a Russian freight company based at Ulyanovsk with a pair of An-124s. Pictured at Palma, Majorca in September 2000 is Antonov An-124-100 Ruslan RA-82003 (c/n 19530502792). It is on lease to Volga-Dnepr Airlines. Later the same year the carrier suspended operations.

Above right: **Trans Oriente** (Transporte Aereo Regular Secundario Oriental SA) is a Colombian mixed freight and passenger carrier with a fleet of five Dornier twin-engine utility aircraft. Dornier Do 28D-2 HK-3991 (c/n 4148) is seen at base, Villavicencio in September 1997.

Right: **Tuninter** is a subsidiary of the Tunisian national flag carrier Tunisair. Boeing 737-3Y0 TS-IEB (c/n 24905) is seen at Frankfurt in June 2001.

Left: Russian passenger carrier Transaero Airlines was one of the first operators in the country to have a largely western-built fleet. Boeing 737-7K9 N100UN (c/n 28088) is seen at Frankfurt in June 2001. It wears the titles Transaero 2000, the name being used at that time.

Below left: Part of the Thomas Cook group, the well-known German holiday charter carrier Condor has now added the parent company name as the main title on its aircraft. Airbus A320-212 D-AICC (c/n 809) is seen at Berlin-Tegel in May 2004.

Below right: In the UK Thomas Cook Airlines is the new operating name for JMC Airlines. Note the different livery from the German division. Stretched Boeing 757-3CQ G-JMAA (c/n 32241) is seen at Manchester in April 2004.

Above left: A member of Grupo TACA, TACA Peru has been set up to operate scheduled passenger services within the country. Airbus A319-132 N471TA (c/n 1066) is seen at its Lima base in October 2003.

Above right: The new generation of water bomber should have been turboprop-powered. Lockheed C-130A Hercules N117TG (c/n 1A-3018) of T & G Aviation is seen at the company base, Chandler-Memorial, Arizona in October 1998. Accidents in 2003 have put a ban on any 'A' model Hercules being given contracts.

Right: Showing off its bright colours at Liverpool in April 1982, is Fairchild FH-227 F-GCLP (c/n 564) of French regional carrier TAT – Touraine Air Transport. Later TAT-European, it merged into Air Liberté in October 1997.

Above: Pictured at Lyon in May 1997, is Beech 1900C-1 Airliner F-GLPK (c/n UC-74). It is marked for **TAT – European Airlines** as well as its owner, Flandre Air, which operates some flights for them. (JDS)

Below: The perfect name for the only airline flying the Scottish Aviation Twin Pioneer on regular services has to be Australia's **Twin Pionair Airlines**. Pictured at the company base, Coolangatta, Queensland in February 2003 is VH-AIS (c/n 540).

Tyumen Avia Trans of Surgut was a Russian general-purpose carrier operating such diverse types as An-2 crop-sprayers and Mil-26 giant helicopters. Yakovlev Yak-40 RA-87343 (c/n 9511239) is seen at Moscow-Vnukovo in August 1997. The carrier was renamed UTair in October 2002. (JDS)

Tyumen Airlines was a mixed passenger and cargo carrier based at Tyumen-Roshino. Tupolev Tu-154B-2 RA-85502 (c/n 502) is seen at Sharjah, UAE in March 2000. The carrier suspended operations in 2003.

Right: Based at Prince Rupert, British Columbia, **Trans Provincial Airlines** had a mixed fleet from a Beaver to a CV-580 via a Bristol Freighter. Pictured at Vancouver in August 1992, is Convair CV-580 C-GKFP (c/n 168). Operations were suspended in March of the following year. (RO'B)

Below: Tampa (Transportes Aereos Mercantiles Panamericanos SA) is a Colombian cargo company based at Medellin. Pictured lined up ready to depart runway 9R at Miami in October 1998 is Douglas DC-8-71F HK-3785X (c/n 46066).

American charter operator **TransMeridian Airlines** was a subsidiary of Irish airline TransAer. Boeing 727-251 N281US (c/n 21160) is seen landing at Miami in October 1998. Following mounting losses the carrier went into Chapter 11 bankruptcy protection in late 2000. Operations still continue.

The national flag carrier, Uganda Airlines, was a very small operation with just domestic and regional international services flown. Pictured at its Entebbe base in November 1997 is leased Boeing 737-2N0 Z-WPA (c/n 23677). The carrier sold its only aircraft, a Fokker F.27, in 2000 and ceased operations. (RO'B)

UAE – Sharjah Ruler's Flight operate VIP services for the Emir. Pictured climbing out of base in March 2000 is Boeing 737-2W8 A6-ESJ (c/n 22628). This has a corporate/VIP interior.

Above: Largest aircraft in the UPS Airlines fleet is the cargo jumbo. Boeing 747-212B N522UP (c/n 21936) is seen on a refuelling stop at Anchorage, Alaska, in May 2000.

Below: UPS Airlines is the flying division of United Parcel Service, one of the largest package carriers in the world. Aircraft of all sizes are flown. Swearingen SA-227AT Expediter N566UP (c/n AT-566) is pictured at Winnipeg in June 1990.

Union Flights is an American small-freight carrier. In addition to normal charters, operations are flown to provide feeder services for the major parcel movers. Beech H18 Tri-gear N7969K (c/n BA-702) is seen at base, Sacramento Executive, in September 1988.

Above left: Ukrainian Cargo Airways is an all-freight carrier based at Zaporozhye. Ilyushin IL-76MD UR-UCH (c/n 0083484536) is seen on a charter supporting the Ukrainian Air Force at Fairford in July 1998.

Above right: US Airways is one of the largest American domestic carriers, and is also expanding the number of European destinations served. Airbus A330-323 N672UW (c/n 333) is pictured arriving at Manchester's Terminal 2 in April 2001.

Left: US Air Express operates commuter and feeder routes. De Havilland Canada DHC-8 Dash 8-202 N987HA (c/n 425) is pictured landing at Miami in October 1998. This aircraft is operated by Piedmont Airlines, a subsidiary of US Air.

Right: Showing a revised colour scheme is one of the western imports to Uzbekistan Airways. Boeing 767-33P(ER) VP-BUZ (c/n 28392) is seen taking off from Sharjah, UAE in March 2000.

Below left: Uzbekistan Airways is the national airline from the former Soviet republic. It has a fleet mix of Russian and western aircraft. Ilyushin IL-86 UK-86056 (c/n 51483203023) is at Sharjah, UAE in March 2000. This design was the only Russian twin-aisle aircraft.

Below right: This Uzbekistan Cargo Antonov An-12B freighter shows a third version of the airline's livery. UK-11369 (c/n 6343810) is seen at Sharjah, UAE in March 2000.

Above: When all its deliveries of the single-aisle Airbus range are completed **United Airlines** will have nearly 200 examples of the type. Airbus A320-232 N430UA (c/n 568) shows the carrier's new livery at Phoenix, Arizona in October 1998.

Below: **United Airlines** is one of the largest carriers in the world, with an extensive US domestic network and flights worldwide. McDonnell Douglas DC-10-10 N1843U (c/n 46636) is seen landing at Los Angeles-LAX in September 1988.

Above: One of the largest commuter types operated by **United Express** was the BAe ATP. N859AW (c/n 2036), which has a 64-seat configuration, is seen at Chicago-O'Hare in September 1992. (RO'B)

Below: **United Express** is the commuter and feeder arm of the company. Shorts SD.360 N622FB (c/n SH3622) lands at Santa Barbara, California in September 1988.

United Shuttle was a low-cost domestic subsidiary of United. Boeing 737-322 N376UA (c/n 24641) is seen arriving at Tucson, Arizona in October 1998, in the revised livery of the division. This internal division of the company was closed in October 2001.

Left: Vietnam Airlines have totally changed their fleet to western designs. Pictured, in the latest livery, is Boeing 767-352(ER) VN-A763 (c/n 26261) as it is pushed back from its gate at Melbourne-Tullamarine in February 2003.

Below left: It is a rare occurrence when a government-owned airline closes down. This happened in 1997 when, following mounting losses, the Venezuelan flag carrier Viasa (Venezolana Internacional de Aviacion) ceased operations. Airbus A300B4-203 YV-161C (c/n 075) is seen at Caracas in November 1992.

Below right: V Bird Airlines was a short-lived Dutch low-cost carrier based at Niederrhein. Airbus A320-212 PH-VAD (c/n 525) is seen at Berlin-Schönefeld in May 2004. All services were suspended in the following October.

Above left: Vipair Airlines was a Kazakh company based at Astana. Seen in a very smart livery is Tupolev Tu-154M UN-85782 (c/n 966) at Frankfurt in June 1999. Later that year the carrier suspended services with the intention to restart.

Above right: Singapore-based start-up Valuair is a low-cost regional passenger carrier. Airbus A320-232 9V-VLA (c/n 2156) is seen at its Changi base in August 2004. (RO'B)

Right: São Paulo is the base of Brazilian airline VASP (Viacao Aerea São Paulo). The carrier operates both domestic and international flights. McDonnell Douglas MD-11 PP-SPK (c/n 48744) lands at Frankfurt in June 1999.

Above left: Voronezhavia was a Russian mixed-role operator from the town of Voronezh. Agriculture featured in many of the carrier's operations. Tupolev Tu-134A-3 RA-65762 (c/n 62279) is seen at Moscow-Vnukovo in August 1997. The airline suspended its services in 2003. (JDS)

Above right: Virgin Atlantic is a British scheduled carrier with an expanding worldwide route network. Pictured at Tokyo-Narita in October 2004 is the ultra-long Airbus A340-642 G-VFOX (c/n 449) as it arrives at its gate following a flight from London.

Right: Virgin Sun was the airline that operated the short-haul routes of Virgin Holidays. The carrier's livery was very bright to reflect its role. Airbus A320-214 G-VMED (c/n 978) lands at Palma Majorca in September 2000. In October 2001 the carrier suspended services.

Above left: Volareweb.com was the marketing name for the low-cost arm of Italian carrier Volare Airlines. The aircraft were painted in a special livery. Airbus A320-212 I-PEKW (c/n 814) is seen at Naples in September 2004. Operations were suspended in November of the same year.

Above right: Virgin Express is the low-cost high-frequency European scheduled operation. Based at Brussels, it has an all-737 fleet. Boeing 737-3Y0 OO-LTV (c/n 23924) is seen arriving at London-Gatwick in August 1998.

Right: Virgin Blue is the Australian low-cost carrier set up by the UK Virgin group. It is one of the fastest growing airlines in the Pacific Rim region. Boeing 737-81Q VH-VOJ (c/n 30787) is seen at the company base, Brisbane, in February 2003. Note the prominent winglets.

Right: Based at the Moscow airport of its name, **Vnukovo Airlines** was one of the first operators of the newer Russian airliner designs. Tupolev Tu-204 RA-64013 (c/n 145743164013) is seen at Moscow-Zhukovsky in August 1995. This aircraft has 210 seats in a one-class configuration. The carrier suspended operations in 2001.

Below: **VARIG Brasil** is one of several long-established South America airlines, having started in 1927. Rio de Janeiro-based, it is the largest airline in Brazil and has an all-American-built fleet. Boeing 767-241 PP-VNR (c/n 23805) arrives at Miami in October 1998.

Above: Antwerp-based **VLM Airlines** (Wings of Flanders) is a Belgian regional carrier with a fleet of Fokker 50s. OO-VLX (c/n 20177) is seen landing at Liverpool, in the new livery of the company, on a service from London-City Airport.

Below: **Veteran Airlines** is a Ukrainian cargo carrier based at Dzhankoi. Pictured making an airshow flypast at Coventry, in August 1999, is Antonov An-12AP UR-PAS (c/n 2401105). (SGW)

Above: **VIP – Vuelos Internos Privados** is a small Ecuadorean airline with a single 32-seat aircraft. Dornier Do 328-120 HC-BXO (c/n 3076) is seen at the company base, Quito, in September 1997.

Right: The '4K' registration on this **Veteran Airlines** Ilyushin IL-76MD indicates that it is on lease to IMAIR of Baku, Azerbaijan. 4K-76717 (c/n 0073474216) is seen at Sharjah, UAE in March 1997.

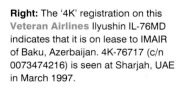

Russian carrier **Volga-Dnepr Airlines** is based at Ulyanovsk-Vostochny. The company has a small passenger division but it is best known for cargo operations on a worldwide basis flying the giant Ruslan freighter. Antonov An-124 RA-82043 (c/n 9773054155101) is pictured as it approaches to land at Osaka-Kansai in October 2004.

Based in the far east of that vast country, Russian carrier **Vladivostok Air** operates both domestic flights to their west and international ones to their east. Tupolev Tu-154M RA-85676 (c/n 836) is seen in Japan at Osaka-Kansai Airport in October 2004.

Left: Based in the northern Italian town of Verona, **Volare Airlines** had a predominantly Airbus fleet. Seen arriving at Manchester, in May 2003, on a football charter is Airbus A321-211 I-PEKM (c/n 1451). Operations were suspended in November 2004.

Right: **Wardair Canada** was one of that nation's leading charter operators and, later, scheduled passenger carriers. Boeing 707-396C C-FZYP (c/n 20043) is seen at Prestwick, Scotland in October 1976. The airline was absorbed into Canadian Airlines in 1990.

Below: **WDL Aviation** is a German freight and passenger company based at Cologne. Fokker F.27-600 Friendship D-AISY (c/n 10391) is seen lining up to depart at Liverpool Airport in July 2004. (JDS)

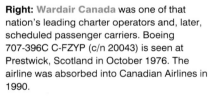

Until it was taken over by Delta in 1987 **Western Airlines** could claim to be one of the oldest US carriers, having been set up in 1925. Boeing 737-247 N4514W (c/n 19611) is seen at San Francisco in October 1979.

Winair was a Salt Lake City-based charter and scheduled carrier. Operations with an all-737 fleet commenced late in 1997. Boeing 737-2Y5 N921WA (c/n 23039) is seen at Miami in October 1998. Operations were suspended in July of the following year.

Above: Calgary-based **Westjet Airlines** is a fast-growing Canadian low-cost high-frequency passenger carrier. It flies an all-737 fleet. Boeing 737-284 C-GGWJ (c/n 21500) is seen at Kelowna, British Columbia in May 2000.

Right: **Woods Air Service** was an Alaskan freight and charter operator. Douglas DC-3 N50CM (c/n 13445) is seen at their Palmer base in May 2000. The company is associated with Woods Air Fuels. Both operations were suspended the following October.

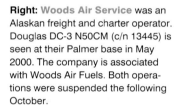

Above left: Based in the city of their name, **Wuhan Airlines** was a Chinese domestic carrier. They had a fleet mix of both Chinese and American built types. Boeing 737-36R B-2988 (c/n 29087) is seen at Guangzhou in October 1999. The carrier was merged into China Eastern Airlines in 2003.

Above right: **West Coast Air** is an all-floatplane operation based at Vancouver Harbour. Services are flown to such locations as Vancouver Island. De Havilland Canada DHC-6 Twin Otter 100 C-GGAW (c/n 86) is seen at base in May 2000.

Left: **Warbelow's Air Ventures** is a Fairbanks, Alaska-based commuter and charter company. The backbone of the fleet is ten Navajos. Piper PA-31-350 Navajo Chieftain N4434D (c/n 31-7552020) is pictured at base in May 2000.

Fairbanks-based **Wright Air Service** is an Alaskan all-purpose passenger and cargo operator. Some of the mixed fleet are ski- and float-equipped. Cessna 208B Grand Caravan N900WA (c/n 208B-0659) is seen at base in May 2000.

Westex Airlines is a Canadian cargo carrier. A number of its aircraft are dedicated to operations for specific parcel companies. Fairchild F-27F C-FVQE (c/n 89) is seen at Vancouver in June 2000. (RO'B)

Above left: **Whitaker Air Charters** of Queensland, Australia have this de Havilland Canada DHC-6 Twin Otter painted in the name of *Lady Elliot Island Reef Resort*, one of their most popular destinations. VH-TZR (c/n 145) is at its Coolangatta base in February 2003.

Above right: Canadian floatplane operator **Wilderness Air** is one of many that fly tourists, especially fishermen, to remote lakeside lodges. De Havilland Canada DHC-3 Otter C-FODV (c/n 411) has cut its engine and floats to the jetty at the company's Vermilion Bay, Ontario base in June 1990.

Left: **Worldways Canada** was a charter operator from Toronto. Formed in 1974, it took that name in 1980. Douglas DC-8-63 C-FCPO (c/n 45926) is seen at base in June 1990. Operations ceased in October of that year, restarted in December, and finally closed down early in 1991.

Below: Norwegian commuter airline **Wideroe** was founded as long ago as 1934. The carrier is associated with SAS. DHC-8-402 Dash 8-Q400 LN-WDC (c/n 4071) is pictured at Manchester in July 2004..

Right: XP Express Parcel Systems is one of the marketing names for TNT. Seen at Liverpool in June 1996, is BAe 146-300QT G-TNTR (c/n E3151). It is in the XP livery.

Below: Xinjiang General Aviation is a Chinese agricultural and utility operator based at Shihezi. Harbin Y-11 B-3870 (c/n 0502) is seen at base in October 1999. This aircraft is a Chinese-designed and built utility passenger and light cargo machine.

Chinese scheduled passenger carrier Xiamen Airlines is based in the city of that name. The fleet is an all-Boeing one of 737 and 757 airliners. New-generation Boeing 737-75C B-2992 (c/n 29086) is pictured at Guangzhou in October 1999.

Yemenia is the only commercial carrier in this Arab country. The fleet mix ranges from a Twin Otter to an IL-76. Boeing 727-2N8 7O-ACX (c/n 21846) arrives at London-Heathrow in July 1996.

Above: Russian mixed fleet carrier, Yamal Airlines is based in Salekhard. Antonov An-74-200 RA-74027 (c/n 36547096920) is seen at Moscow-Domodedovo in August 2004. This aircraft is flown as a freighter. (SGW)

Right: Yana Airlines was a Cambodian carrier operating charter flights from Phnom Penh. Services commenced at the end of 1998. Ilyushin IL-62M XU-229 (c/n 4445032) is seen at Sharjah, UAE in March 2000. The carrier was renamed Mekong Airlines.

Above: Based at Zhengzhou, Chinese passenger airline **Zhongyuan Airlines** was formed in 1986 as the carrier for the province of Henan. Boeing 737-37K B-2935 (c/n 27283) is seen at Beijing in October 1999. The company was merged into China Southern Airlines in 2002.

Right: **Zantop International Airlines** was a cargo carrier based at Detroit-Willow Run, specialising in motor industry work. Lockheed L-188AF Electra N341HA (c/n 1035) is pictured with its engines running at base in June 1990. Since 1997 both the company and its aircraft have been offered for sale, limited operations continue.

Below: Pictured at Harare, Zimbabwe, on a local international flight in April 1993 is Boeing 737-2M9 9J-AEG (c/n 21236) of **Zambia Airways**. This operator was the national flag carrier and ceased services the following year. The name has since been taken by a new Lusaka-based small carrier. (RO'B)

Canadian charter carrier **Zoom Airlines** flies holidaymakers to Europe with a pair of 767s. Pictured at Manchester in June 2003, is Boeing 767-328(ER) C-GZUM (c/n 27135) in a very distinctive livery.

Special Colour Schemes

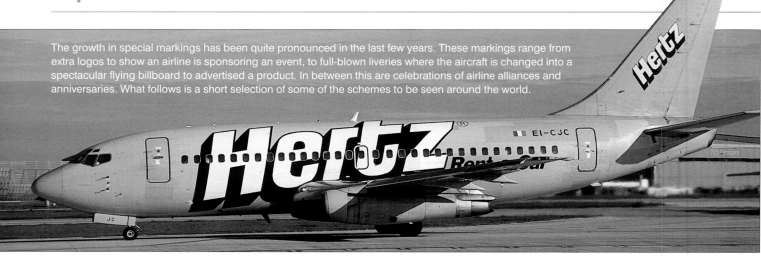

The growth in special markings has been quite pronounced in the last few years. These markings range from extra logos to show an airline is sponsoring an event, to full-blown liveries where the aircraft is changed into a spectacular flying billboard to advertised a product. In between this are celebrations of airline alliances and anniversaries. What follows is a short selection of some of the schemes to be seen around the world.

Sydney was the setting for the year 2000 Olympic summer games. **Ansett Australia** was the official airline and they decorated this Boeing 737-33A VH-CZT (c/n 27454). Pictured at Sydney in October 2000, it has the three mascots of the games, Syd, Millie and Olly, on the rear fuselage. (RO'B)

Above: Another example of an **Air Portugal** special scheme is Boeing 737-382 CS-TIB (c/n 24365). This is marked to advertise 'Expo 98' being held in Lisbon. It is seen at Zürich in June 1997. (JDS)

Above: 'Hertz Rent-a-Car' is the billboard advertising on this **Ryanair** aircraft. Boeing 737-204 EI-CJC (c/n 22640) is seen at Manchester in April 2004.

Seen at Zürich in June 1997, is **Air Portugal** Boeing 737-382 CS-TIC (c/n 24366). Its extra colours and titles 'Fly Algarve' relate to the coastal holiday area of the country. (JDS)

Italian carrier **Alpi Eagles** has several of their fleet of Fokker 100s painted to advertise Jolly Motor, a racing team of boats. I-ALPW (c/n 11255) is seen at Naples in September 2004.

Right: Seen departing Quito, Ecuador in September 1997 is **Avianca** Boeing 727-2H3 HK-3480X (c/n 20739). It has an all-red fuselage and advertises financial institute 'Bancoquia'.

Rare original short-body Boeing 737-112 N708AW (c/n 19771) of **America West** has extra titles promoting the 'Phoenix Suns', a local basketball team. The aircraft is seen on the move at Phoenix in October 1998.

The airlines in the 'Star Alliance' group of carriers usually have at least one aircraft in each of their fleets specially marked to show membership. Boeing 767-381 JA8290 (c/n 24417) of **All Nippon Airways** is seen at Osaka-Itami in October 2004. It is of note that it still carries the logo of Ansett Australia three years after that company ceased operations.

Above left: **Alitalia** Boeing 747-243B I-DEMS (c/n 22969) was a flying advertisement for Bulgari watches, with a striking aluminium finish. It was photographed at Bangkok in November 1999.

Above right: Japanese carrier **All Nippon Airways** has several aircraft painted with cartoon characters. Boeing 747-481 JA8962 (c/n 25644) has 'Pocket Monsters' livery. It is seen landing at Tokyo-Narita Airport in October 2004.

Left: A far more lavish paintwork for the 'Pokemon' cartoon characters adorns this **All Nippon Airways** Jumbo. Boeing 747-481D JA8957 (c/n 25642) is seen at Okinawa in October 2004. This aircraft is one of the fleet of 'domestic' Jumbos. It has a seating capacity of 569 and, unlike most '400' series 747s, does not have winglets.

Trigema is a German sports wear manufacturer. It has used **Aero Lloyd** Airbus A321-231 D-ALAH (c/n 792) as a flying billboard. The aircraft is seen at Frankfurt in June 1999.

Hong Kong-based **Cathay Pacific** has painted this aircraft to celebrate their home city. Boeing 747-467 B-HOX (c/n 24955) is seen at base in March 2003.

Australia's Qantas has painted a number of both long- and short-haul aircraft in special markings. Boeing 747-338 VH-EBU (c/n 23223) has the 'Nalangi Dreaming' blue coral fish scheme. It is pictured at Brisbane in February 2003.

Motor racing's 'Formula 1' is a worldwide brand; to advertise the Australian Grand Prix Qantas painted extra markings on this Jumbo. Boeing 747-438 VH-OJC (c/n 24406) is seen at Bangkok in February 2001.

Above left: Qantas has painted a complete 747 in an Aboriginal-style colour scheme. Boeing 747-438 VH-OJB (c/n 24373) is seen landing at London-Heathrow in June 2000. This design from the Balarinji studio was also used by British Airways as one of its tail markings. It was to symbolise the relationship between the two carriers. (SGW)

Above right: This Qantas Boeing 737-838 VH-VXB (c/n 30101) has the 'Yanani Dreaming' scheme. It is seen at Melbourne-Tullamarine in February 2003.

Left: Another Crossair SAAB 2000, HB-IYD (c/n 2000-059), was part of the Swiss bid to hold the Winter Olympics at Sion in 2006. The markings were removed when the town lost its games bid. The aircraft is pictured on a regular scheduled service to Manchester in April 1999.

Air Europa publicises the Andalucia region of Spain with titles on Boeing 737-4Q8 EC-FXQ (c/n 24707). It is seen landing at Madrid in September 2002.

'The Phantom of the Opera' is a musical being performed at many locations around the world. To advertise the production in the Swiss city of Berne, Crossair has applied special livery to SAAB 2000 HB-IZK (c/n 2000-018). It is seen at Zürich in June 1997. (JDS)

Above left: Norwegian airline Braathens has put its web address on this 737 in place of traditional titles. Boeing 737-405 LN-BUF (c/n 25795) is seen approaching London-Gatwick in August 1997.

Above right: German carrier LTU has an aircraft painted to advertise 'Hertha BSC Berlin', a football team. Airbus A320-214 D-ALTD (c/n 1493) is seen arriving at Manchester in May 2003 with a planeload of Italian football fans.

Left: To advertise the Winter Olympics at Salt Lake City in 2002, Delta Air Lines produced a special scheme. Called 'The Soaring Spirit', it showed a speed skater on the fin. Boeing 777-232(ER) N864DA (c/n 29736) is seen at Manchester in April 2002.

Right: Wearing the 'Rizzi Bird' scheme, this Condor Boeing 757-230 D-ABNF (c/n 25140) is at Cologne-Bonn in May 1997. The markings are in the style of children's drawings. (JDS)

Below left: Germania Airlines has painted several aircraft in the markings of some of the tour and holiday companies it flies for. D-AGES Boeing 737-75B (c/n 28108) is 'Jahn Reisen'. It is pictured at Palma, Majorca in September 2000.

Below right: Emerald Airways showed it had a contract for postal deliveries by painting a 748 with 'Royal Mail Skynet' titles on an all-red aircraft. Hawker Siddeley (Avro) 748-105 Srs.1 G-BEJE (c/n 1556) is seen at its Liverpool base in June 1996.

Boeing 737-75B D-AGEN (c/n 28100) of Germania is seen in the distinctive markings of 'TUI' at Palma, Majorca in September 2000.

'Tjaereborg' markings adorn this Germania Boeing 737-75B. D-AGER (c/n 28107) is seen at Palma, Majorca in September 2000.

Right: The Chinese are promoting the island of Hainan, off the southern coast, as a tropical holiday resort. To reflect this Hainan Airlines has painted its aircraft in special markings. Boeing 737-84P B-2647 (c/n 29947) is seen at Guangzhou in October 1999, showing blue sea together with seashells and fish.

Below: Hawaiian Airlines can be proud of a seventy-year history. To commemorate this McDonnell Douglas DC-10-30 N68060 (c/n 47850) was specially painted. It is seen at Los Angeles-LAX in June 2000. (RO'B)

Above: This Hainan Airlines Boeing 737-3Q8 B-2938 (c/n 26296) is seen wearing tropical flowers as it arrives at Beijing in October 1999.

Below: Lufthansa Cargo has painted this Boeing 747-230F to show times and locations around the world and how cargo flights can connect them. D-ABZF (c/n 23621) is seen at Sharjah, UAE in March 2000.

Rugby football is the theme of this Impulse Airlines Beech 1900D Airliner VH-IMQ (c/n UE-273). It was photographed at Sydney in October 2000. (RO'B)

Above left: Belgian financial newspaper 'De Tijd' is advertised on this **VLM** Fokker 50. OO-VLM is seen at Manchester in August 2003.

Above right: One of the closest working relationships between two airlines is that of **Northwest Airlines** and KLM. To highlight this, Northwest has painted McDonnell Douglas DC-10-30 N237NW (c/n 47844) in joint colours. It is seen at Amsterdam-Schiphol in October 1999.

Left: **South African Airways** has painted this Jumbo in specialised 'Olympic Team' colours. Boeing 747-312 ZS-SAJ (c/n 23027) is seen at Cape Town in October 2002. (RO'B)

Above left: Irish carrier **Ryanair** has a number of its aircraft decorated in flying billboard schemes. Boeing 737-230 EI-CNY (c/n 22113) lands at London-Gatwick in August 1998 in a scheme advertising 'Kilkenny, the cream of Irish beer'. Note how the cockpit has the white head of the drink.

Above right: Irish mobile telephone company 'Eircell' have special colours on this **Ryanair** aircraft. Boeing 737-204 EI-CJD (c/n 22966) is seen on approach to Manchester in March 2002.

Right: A pat on the back. For five years running **Southwest Airlines** have been listed by the US Department of Transport as having the best on-time performance, best baggage handling and fewest complaints of any major carrier. Boeing 737-3H4 N647SW (c/n 27717) was delivered as the 'Triple Crown'. It is seen at Phoenix in October 1998.

Many of **Southwest Airlines** flights operate to Arizona. To acknowledge this Boeing 737-3H4 N383SW (c/n 26589) wears the colours of the state's flag. It is pictured at Dallas-Love Field in October 1998.

Singapore Airlines introduced 'Tropical Megatop' colours on the Boeing 747-412 9V-SPL (c/n 26557) to launch the upgrading of its three classes of service. It is seen at Manchester in October 1999. (RO'B)

Thai Airways has one of the best special schemes currently seen. It features a Royal Barge and is to promote tourism in the country. Airbus A330-322 HS-TEK (c/n 244) is seen at Bangkok in February 2001.

Above: In the football World Cup year of 1998, Brazilian carrier **TAM** painted Fokker 100 PT-MRX (c/n 11341) in national colours. It is seen at São Paulo in October 1998. (RO'B)

Left: Showing a red fuselage painted with white aircraft silhouettes is **SAS** McDonnell Douglas MD-82 LN-RLE (c/n 49382) as it takes off from Palma, Majorca in September 2000. The carrier has decorated another aircraft in a blue and white version of this scheme.

Below: Brazilian carrier **VARIG** painted McDonnell Douglas MD-11 PP-VPP (c/n 48501) for the transport of the national football team to the 1998 World Cup tournament in France. It is pictured landing at London-Heathrow in July 1999.

Russian carrier **Transaero** applied '850 Years of Moscow' titles to Ilyushin IL-86 RA-86123 (c/n 51483210091). It is seen at Moscow-Sheremetyevo in August 1997. (JDS)

Tails of British Airways

Having had the same livery since 1984, British Airways decided in 1995 to have a new image. The contract winner was the London-based Newell and Sorrell company, whose idea was quite revolutionary for an airline, as it featured a standard fuselage marking with the company name but with a variety of tails. These tail markings, of which fifty were planned, were designed by commercial and ethnic artists from around the world. The aim was to highlight the fact that BA is a global carrier.

When in June 1997, the schemes were unveiled, there seemed to be no middle ground: people either loved them or hated them with a passion. Most famous of the latter was the former Prime Minister Lady Thatcher, who publicly covered a model of one of the schemes with her handkerchief. Most of the objections revolved around the fact that the new image did not show the Union Jack flag, even though, it has to be said, the previous livery only had a stylised flag.

After two years of the new image, the groundswell of opinion, coupled with poor operating profits and the sacking of the chief executive, had its effect. The company announced it would put all new aircraft in the one scheme featuring the flag, this having been originally reserved for the Concorde fleet only. It would also over the next few years, repaint the aircraft that were in the 'World Images' livery to make them once again 'fly the flag'.

The photographs that follow show a cross section of the schemes and the BA types in service with them, together with some franchise-operated aircraft which also wear the colours.

Animals and Trees is from a painting by Cg'ose Ntcox'o, an artist from the Ncoakhoe tribe of the San people who live in the Kalahari Desert of Botswana and was carried by Boeing 737-236 G-BGDT (c/n 21807).

Nami Tsuru or 'waves and cranes' is a Japanese design from the artist Matazo Kayama. It appears on Boeing 737-236 G-BKYP (c/n 23226) seen landing at Manchester in April 1998.

China is represented by **Rendezvous**. It is designed by Yip Man-Yam, a calligrapher from Hong Kong, and is a poem on the subject of how to make a cup of tea. It is seen on Boeing 737-37Q G-OAMS (c/n 28548) at Manchester in May 1998.

A Scottish tartan designed by weaver Peter MacDonald is called **Benyhone,** or 'Mountain of the Birds'. It features on Boeing 737-436 G-DOCJ (c/n 25840) seen at Manchester in March 1999.

From Ireland comes **Colum** or 'Dove'. Designed by Timothy O'Neill it draws inspiration from the ancient Book of Kells. Boeing 737-34S G-OGBB (c/n 29108) wears it at London-Gatwick in August 1998.

Vinger 'Wings' is a Danish design showing seagulls in flight. The artist is Per Arnoldi. It is seen on Boeing 737-4S3 G-BUHL (c/n 25134) at London-Gatwick in August 1998.

Above: Antje Bruggeman, a German artist, produced Bauhaus. Originally for Deutsche BA, it has since joined the main fleet. Boeing 737-36Q G-OFRA (c/n 29327) is seen at Manchester in March 1999.

Below: English design Grand Union is by Christine Bass. It is based on colour schemes painted on narrow boats on the Grand Union Canal. Boeing 737-36N G-XBHX (c/n 28572) is seen at Manchester in March 1999.

Above: Golden Khokhloma is a Russian design by village artist Taisia Akimovna Belyantzeva. Its pattern represents fruit and flowers used to decorate utensils in the region of the mid-Volga. Boeing 737-36N G-XMAN (c/n 28573) is seen at Manchester in June 1999.

Below: Seen landing at Zürich in August 1998, is Boeing 757-236 G-BMRG (c/n 24102). This has a one-off variant of the Chinese Rendezvous scheme. It has a cream background, not a white one.

Above: South Africa is the home of the Ndebele design, originated by sisters Emmly and Martha Masanabo. The two schemes appear similar but are not identical. Boeing 747-436 G-BNLJ (c/n 24052) is seen at London-Heathrow in July 1999, wearing Martha's version.

Below: Indian design Paithani is featured on Boeing 747-236B G-BDXO (c/n 23799) at London-Heathrow, July 1999. Textile artist Meera Mehta produced this from patterns that she uses in the weaving of saris.

Wunala Dreaming is an Australian scheme from the Balarinji studio. It is an Aboriginal design and is also used to cover a complete Qantas 747 (see Special Colours section). It is to mark the co-operation between the two airlines. Boeing 757-236 G-BIFK (c/n 22177) displays it at London-Heathrow in July 1999.

Boeing 767-336 G-BNWB (c/n 24334) at Frankfurt in June 1999, shows the **Chelsea Rose**. This design by Pierce Casey was the winner of a competition run by BA and *The Sunday Times* newspaper.

Above: **Water Dreaming** is another Australian design. This one is by Aboriginal Clifford Possum. The circles represent waterholes. It is seen on Airbus A320-211 G-BUSJ (c/n 109) at London-Heathrow in July 1999.

Below: All new airliner deliveries will feature the **Chatham Union Flag** as a factory-applied marking. Latest type in the fleet, Airbus A319-131 G-EUPB (c/n 1115) is seen landing at Palma, Majorca in September 2000.

Swedish designer Ulrica Hydman-Vallien has produced **Blomsterang** or 'Flower Fields', it features flowers and hearts. Boeing 757-236 G-BMRI (c/n 24267) is seen at London-Heathrow in July 1999.

Above: The **Chatham Union Flag** was originally to be a Concorde-only tail. This, however, will become the standard scheme for the entire passenger fleet. It is based upon a Union Jack flag from the Chatham Naval Dockyard. BAe/Aérospatiale Concorde 102 G-BOAF (c/n 216) is seen landing at Fairford in July 1997.

Below: The Boeing 777-236 is becoming more and more popular in the fleet mix of BA. G-VIIT (c/n 29962) is seen at London-Heathrow in July 1999 in the Chinese **Rendezvous** scheme with the place name Hong Kong now added.

From Polish artist Danuta Wojda comes **Kogutki Lowickie**, 'Cockerel of Lowicz'. It features flowers, peacocks and cockerels in a circular design. Boeing 747-436 G-BNLT (c/n 24630) is seen at London-Heathrow in July 1999.

As well as BA, various franchise operators use the World Image designs on their aircraft. **British Regional Airlines** Embraer RJ 145EU G-EMBD (c/n 145039) has the **Animals and Trees** design from Botswana. It is pictured landing at Manchester in May 1999.

British Regional Airlines BAe ATP G-MAUD (c/n 2002) has the English design, Blue Poole. The artist is Sally Tuffin from Poole Pottery and shows seagulls and dolphins. It is seen at Manchester in May 1998.

Above: Maersk Air of Birmingham was owned by the Danish Maersk group. As a BA franchise operator it used the World Image tail colours. BAe 4100 Jetstream 41 G-MSKJ (c/n 41034) has the South African Ndebele-Martha design at Newcastle in September 1998.

Left: British Mediterranean Airways specialises in services to Beirut and the surrounding region on a regular scheduled basis. It is also a BA franchisee. Airbus A320-231 G-MEDD (c/n 386) has the Egyptian Crossing Borders design by Chant Avedissian, based on a traditional tent hanging. It is pictured at London-Heathrow in July 1999.-

The only Canadair RJs to be seen in BA colours were the Maersk Air ones. Showing the Danish Vinger 'Wings' design is Canadair Regional Jet RJ200LR G-MSKK (c/n 7226) seen at its Birmingham base in August 1999.

CityFlyer Express is a London-Gatwick-based international commuter and regional carrier owned by BA. G-BZAT Avro RJ100 (c/n E3320) features the American Waves of the City tail at its base in August 1998. The designer for this is Jennifer Koblarz and it is said to be sinuous organic lines.

The sight of a 727 in BA colours is an odd one, as it is the only Boeing-designed jet never to appear in BA's fleet. The explanation is that it belongs to South African franchise operator Comair of Johannesburg. Boeing 727-230A ZS-NZV (c/n 20792) is seen at Cape Town in May 2000. It features the Irish designed Colum or 'Dove' scheme. (RO'B)

ATR 72-202 G-BXTN (c/n 483) of CityFlyer Express shows the Canadian design Whale Rider at Düsseldorf in September 1998. The inspiration for this was a painted wood carving by Joe David from the Clayoquot people from the country's north-west coastal region.

Index of Airliner Types

Airbus
A300 10, 13, 19, 20, 23, 41, 46, 51, 53, 62, 67, 71, 74, 76, 78, 79, 96, 106, 110, 124, 131, 140
A300ST Beluga 25
A310 3, 7, 9, 11, 20, 40, 54, 63, 74, 85, 124
A319 11, 45, 63, 105, 111, 115, 135, 157
A320 5, 6, 9, 15, 17, 31, 33, 42, 43, 45, 47, 52, 64, 65, 68, 70, 78, 80, 81, 86, 88, 95, 113, 119, 121, 130, 131, 135, 139, 140, 141, 151, 157, 158
A321 16, 26, 106, 129, 143, 149
A330 14, 20, 39, 45, 57, 110, 115, 122, 130, 138, 154
A340 6, 9, 10, 12, 31, 33, 46, 52, 65, 72, 88, 103, 109, 115, 126, 141
Antonov
An-8 92
An-12 29, 49, 86, 98, 107, 118, 122, 124, 138, 142
An-24 27, 47, 58, 119, 131, 132
An-26 20, 62
An-32 14, 17, 61, 76, 116, 120
An-74 117, 146
An-124 7, 14, 111, 134, 143
Armstrong-Whitworth
Argosy 76
ATR
42 16, 17, 28, 35, 62, 71, 89, 107, 113
72 13, 29, 53, 54, 69, 79, 90, 131, 158
Aviation Traders
ATL.98 Carvair 108

BAC
One-Eleven 9, 18, 36, 39, 40, 96, 100, 128, 129
BAe
146/Avro RJ 4, 6, 24, 41, 42, 43, 44, 51, 57, 62, 78, 90, 93, 101, 105, 110, 115, 119, 146, 158
ATP 4, 43, 63, 139, 158
Jetstream 31/32 3, 5, 99, 102, 133
Jetstream 41 62, 96, 127, 158
BAe/Aérospatiale
Concorde 6, 157
Beech
18 59, 137
1900 13, 34, 42, 66, 124, 136, 152
B200 113
Bell
206L Long Ranger 74
Boeing
377-MG Mini Guppy 18
707 8, 14, 30, 59, 65, 80, 92, 116, 123, 126, 133, 143
717 29, 41, 78, 110, 128
727 3, 15, 16, 18, 21, 25, 27, 28, 40, 42, 44, 47, 50, 56, 66, 79, 82, 86, 92, 97, 98, 102, 107, 109, 112, 117, 120, 121, 123, 126, 131, 132, 136, 146, 148, 158
737 3, 4, 8, 10, 11, 17, 18, 19, 21, 22, 23, 30, 32, 33, 34, 35, 37, 38, 39, 44, 45, 46, 50, 51, 52, 54, 55, 59, 60, 61, 63, 66, 67, 70, 71, 72, 73, 74, 75, 77, 81, 83, 85, 86, 87, 88, 89, 90, 91, 93, 94, 95, 97, 98, 99, 100, 103, 105, 106, 108, 109, 113, 116, 118, 119, 120, 121, 123, 125, 126, 127, 128, 129, 132, 134, 135, 137, 139, 141, 143, 144, 146, 147, 148, 149, 150, 151, 152, 153, 154, 155, 156
747 7, 9, 13, 21, 28, 29, 45, 47, 48, 50, 53, 54, 55, 58, 65, 78, 80, 81, 84, 85, 94, 95, 98, 100, 101, 103, 105, 118, 125, 126, 128, 130, 137, 149, 150, 152, 153, 154, 156, 157
747SP 21, 32, 45, 114, 122
757 5, 13, 15, 22, 44, 45, 53, 56, 60, 61, 66, 68, 69, 70, 72, 75, 77, 89, 92, 97, 100, 112, 113, 116, 120, 130, 135, 151, 156, 157
767 3, 11, 12, 15, 22, 24, 36, 55, 56, 64, 87, 91, 123, 127, 129, 132, 138, 140, 142, 147, 149, 157
777 5, 6, 7, 24, 28, 46, 53, 79, 84, 85, 87, 95, 104, 114, 126, 151, 157
C-97 73
Bristol
170 39, 76
Britten-Norman
Islander 86, 113
Trislander 10, 47
Canadair
CL-44 14
CL-215 34
Regional Jet 6, 18, 24, 25, 31, 37, 49, 70, 81, 94, 127, 158
CASA
212 41
Cessna
185 89
208 48, 60, 82, 107, 130, 145
310 76
402 11
Convair
CV-340 50
CV-440 30, 112, 129
CV-580 15, 49, 136
Curtiss
C-46 5, 17, 32, 38, 61

Dassault
Falcon 20 60
De Havilland
DH.89A Dragon Rapide 114
DH.104 Dove 49, 93
DH.106 Comet 57
De Havilland Australia
DHA-3 Drover 43
De Havilland Canada
DHC-2 Beaver 36, 111, 133
DHC-3 Otter 14, 71, 73, 97, 145
DHC-4 Caribou 19
DHC-6 Twin Otter 10, 25, 26, 35, 88, 93, 124, 144, 145
DHC-7 Dash 7 71
DHC-8 Dash 8 7, 11, 18, 23, 27, 38, 44, 55, 58, 65, 72, 73, 75, 77, 103, 126, 134, 138, 145
Dornier
Do 28 134
Do 228 89
Do 328 87, 105, 142

Douglas
A-26 Invader 12
C-133 Cargomaster 51
DC-3 20, 21, 26, 27, 30, 57, 59, 61, 63, 89, 92, 93, 108, 118, 124, 144
DC-4 37, 38, 47, 68, 106, 125
DC-6 5, 26, 30, 48, 50, 69, 99, 100, 115
DC-7 77, 121
DC-8 4, 16, 19, 21, 22, 23, 24, 40, 46, 63, 84, 91, 112, 116, 136, 145
DC-9 22, 25, 32, 65, 98, 101
Embraer
EMB-110 Bandeirante 8, 12, 71, 82
EMB-120 Brasilia 55
ERJ 35, 39, 46, 54, 64, 105, 114, 119, 125, 157
Fairchild
C-119 73
F-27 27, 88, 104, 145
FH-227 10, 21, 135
Fokker
50 8, 12, 16, 57, 84, 101, 112, 142, 153
70 46, 128
100 5, 14, 28, 34, 62, 72, 75, 133, 148, 154
F.27 15, 49, 65, 79, 86, 104, 134, 143
F.28 25, 55, 87, 91, 107, 120
GAF
N22 Nomad 127
Grumman
G-73 Mallard 51
S-2 Tracker 50
Harbin
Y-11 146
Hawker Siddeley
748 22, 48, 57, 64, 67, 75, 121, 151
Andover 32, 80
HS.121 Trident 40
Ilyushin
IL-18 31, 58, 76, 77, 124
IL-62 9, 54, 59, 134, 146
IL-76 12, 26, 34, 92, 106, 109, 117, 138, 142
IL-86 33, 53, 104, 138, 154
IL-96 7
Junkers
Ju-52/3M 80
LET
L-410 31, 33
Lockheed
Hercules 3, 87, 104, 114, 127, 135
L-1011 TriStar 15, 20, 36, 41, 49, 68, 78, 84, 104, 111
L-188 Electra 12, 30, 67, 82, 112, 132, 147
P-2 Neptune 93
P-3 Orion 18
Martin
JRM3 Mars 69
McDonnell Douglas
DC-10 23, 42, 44, 50, 61, 64, 72, 86, 97, 133, 139, 152, 153

MD-11 56, 61, 67, 69, 79, 85, 88, 94, 114, 123, 140, 154
MD-81 68, 96
MD-82 29, 32, 38, 154
MD-83 10, 36, 38, 48, 68, 70, 96, 97, 103, 122
MD-88 3
MD-90 19, 52, 56
Mil
Mi-8 94
Mi-17 73
NAMC
YS-11 24
Noorduyn
Norseman 112, 117
Nord
N-262 57, 76
Pilatus
PC-12 87, 98
Piper
PA-23 82
PA-31 34, 37, 43, 74, 132, 144
PZL-Mielec
An-2 111
SAAB
340 25, 29, 69, 81, 100, 111, 122
2000 90, 115, 150
Scottish Aviation
Twin Pioneer 136
Shorts
SC.5 Belfast 74
SC.7 Skyvan 31
SD.330 29, 103
SD.360 17, 42, 51, 106, 108, 123, 139
Sikorsky
S-58 41, 132
S-64 64
Sud Aviation
SA.316B Alouette III 26
SE.210 Caravelle 30, 72
Swearingen
Metro 28, 33, 80, 84, 96, 107, 109, 116, 137
Tupolev
Tu-134 24, 28, 33, 34, 38, 48, 54, 82, 102, 108, 130, 141
Tu-154 8, 17, 23, 42, 43, 47, 48, 53, 58, 82, 83, 94, 102, 117, 118, 122, 124, 131, 136, 140, 143
Tu-204 142
Vickers
Vanguard 75
Xian
Y-7 47
Yakovlev
Yak-40 56, 90, 102, 136
Yak-42 4, 20, 24, 52, 83, 85, 120
Yunshuji
Y-5 51
Y-8 49

Bibliography

Books

Piston Engine Airliner Production List (various editions):
Tony Eastwood & John Roach; The Aviation Hobby Shop, London.

Jet Engine Production List Volume 1 & 2 (various editions):
Tony Eastwood & John Roach; The Aviation Hobby Shop, London.

Turbo Prop Airliner Production List (various editions):
Tony Eastwood & John Roach; The Aviation Hobby Shop, London.

JP Airline Fleets: Ulrich Klee; Bucher & Co, Zürich (various editions).

Lockheed 188 Electra: David G Powers; World Transport Press, Miami.

McDonnell Douglas DC-10: Terry Waddington; World Transport Press, Miami.

Magazines

Airliners, Airliner World, Airways, Aviation Letter, Propliner & World Airliner Fleets News (various editions).

We hope you enjoyed this book . . .

Midland Publishing offers an extensive range of outstanding aviation titles, of which a small selection are shown here.

We always welcome ideas from authors or readers for books they would like to see published.

In addition, our associate, Midland Counties Publications, offers an exceptionally wide range of aviation, military, naval and transport books and videos for sale by mail-order worldwide.

For a copy of the appropriate catalogue, or to order further copies of this book, and any other Midland Publishing titles, please write, telephone, fax or e-mail to:

Midland Counties Publications
4 Watling Drive, Hinckley,
Leics, LE10 3EY, England
Tel: (+44) 01455 254 450
Fax: (+44) 01455 233 737
E-mail: midlandbooks@compuserve.com
www.midlandcountiessuperstore.com

US distribution by Specialty Press –
see page 2.

RUSSIAN AIRLINES AND THEIR AIRCRAFT

Dmitriy Komissarov & Yefim Gordon

Following the ending of Aeroflot's monopoly in 1992 and the break-up of the Soviet Union, the Russian civil air transport scene has been considerably transformed.

This full-colour album covers the major airlines operating in Russia today, illustrating the types operated by each carrier, their equipment and the various colour schemes worn by them. A brief history and fleet information are provided for each airline, as are detailed photo captions.

Softback, 280 x 215 mm, 160 pages
449 full colour photographs
1 85780 176 8 **£19.99**

ARRIVALS & DEPARTURES
North American Airlines 1990-2000

John K Morton

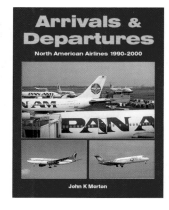

This is a photographic record, with extended captions, of new and departed North American airlines during the last decade of the 20th century. It is divided into three sections: 'Arrivals' contains 32 airlines which began operations during the period and were still operational at the end of it; 'Arrivals and Departures' features 24 carriers which came and went, and 'Departures' covers 29 airlines which went out of business in the 1990s. Included here are famous names such as PanAm, Eastern and Tower Air.

Softback, 280 x 215 mm, 112 pages
168 full colour photographs
1 85780 200 4 **£14.99**

EUROPEAN AIRLINES

John K Morton

This book portrays with extended captions, a broad selection of over 100 primarily passenger-carrying airlines from 33 European countries. Starting in Ireland and continuing around the continent, the reader is taken on a 'tour' of European nations, and in each case liveries of based airlines, including all the major flag carriers, scheduled and charter airlines are included. As wide a variety of types – jets and propliners – as possible are shown and an equally-varied range of colour schemes.

Softback, 280 x 215 mm, 112 pages
c190 full colour photographs
1 85780 210 1 May c**£14.99**

AIRLINERS WORLDWIDE
Over 100 Current Airliners Described and Illustrated in Colour (2nd edition)

Tom Singfield

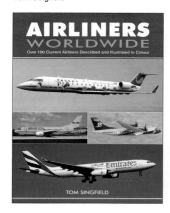

The coverage in this new edition of this valuable guidebook is markedly different, up-to-the-minute and indispensable. The text for each type has been revised and updated. Each type has an historical narrative and description of model variants and type of operations plus principal technical details and a listing of current operators. The photographic selection is all new and types new to this edition include the Embraer 170 and 195, the Antonov An-140, Airbus A318 and A380.

Softback, 240 x 170 mm, 128 pages
136 colour photographs
1 85780 189 X **£13.99**

AIRLINES WORLDWIDE
Over 360 Airlines Described and Illustrated in Colour (4th edition)

B I Hengi

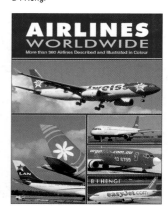

Airlines Worldwide, first published in 1994, has established itself as a trusted and sought-after reference work. It aims to give an overview and illustrate the world's leading or more interesting airlines, including smaller national operators, with their history, routes, aircraft fleet and operations.

This latest edition is more than ever revised and updated, notably in the light of the turbulent events and rapid changes in the airline industry over the past couple of years.

Softback, 240 x 170 mm, 384 pages
c360 colour photographs
1 85780 155 5 **£18.99**

AIRLINES REMEMBERED
Over 200 Airlines of the Past, Described and Illustrated in Colour

B I Hengi

In the same format as the enormously popular *Airlines Worldwide* and *Airlines Worldwide*, this companion reviews the histories and operations of over 200 airlines from the last thirty years which are no longer with us, each illustrated with a full colour photograph showing at least one of their aircraft in the colour scheme of that era. Operators such as BEA, CP Air, Eastern, Invicta, Jet 24, Laker and Fred Olsen are examples of the extensive and varied coverage.

Softback, 240 x 170 mm, 224 pages
c200 colour photographs
1 85780 091 5 **£14.95**

AIRLINERS WORLDWIDE
76 Older Types, Worldwide, Described and Illustrated in Colour

Tom Singfield

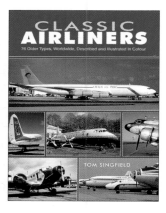

This companion volume reviews the histories, operations and specifications of 76 airliner types which have been familiar during the last fifty years, and includes over 200 outstanding colour photos showing the airliners both in service and preserved. Included are less well-known yet significant types, for instance the Dassault Mercure, Breguet Deux Ponts, Saab Scandia, and VFW-614. Of course, all the appropriate Boeing, Douglas, Antonov, Lockheed, Ilyushin, and Tupolev types appear.

Softback, 240 x 170 mm, 160 pages
over 200 colour photographs
1 85780 098 2 **£13.95**